Thinking by numbers 3

Written by DIANA COBDEN

Series editor STEVE HIGGINS

OXFORD
UNIVERSITY PRESS

OXFORD

UNIVERSITY PRESS

Great Clarendon Street, Oxford OX2 6DP

Oxford University Press is a department of the University of Oxford.
It furthers the University's objective of excellence in research,
scholarship, and education by publishing worldwide in

Oxford   New York

Auckland   Cape Town   Dar es Salaam   Hong Kong   Karachi
Kuala Lumpur   Madrid   Melbourne   Mexico City   Nairobi
New Delhi   Shanghai   Taipei   Toronto

With offices in

Argentina   Austria   Brazil   Chile   Czech Republic   France   Greece
Guatemala   Hungary   Italy   Japan   South Korea   Poland   Portugal
Singapore   Switzerland   Thailand   Turkey   Ukraine   Vietnam

Oxford is a registered trade mark of Oxford University Press
in the UK and in certain other countries

British Library Cataloguing in Publication Data

Data available

ISBN-13: 9780198361251
ISBN-10: 019 836125 4

3 5 7 9 10 8 6 4 2

Illustrated by Andrew Keylock
Typeset by Artistix, Thame, Oxon
Printed in Great Britain by Ashford Colour Press, Gosport, Hants

Contents

Introduction

Thinking by Numbers aims to develop thinking skills through mathematics lessons and activities across the primary age range. Although it can be used by an individual teacher, we think that you will get the best from the series if you use the activities across your school to undertake a professional inquiry into the potential of these lessons to develop pupils' thinking. Hence, the sections on *Professional development* (page 9), *Classroom management* (page 12), *Formative assessment and assessment for learning* (page 14), and *Speaking and listening* (page 18) are important aspects of the series. These sections will support you in helping to make the activities successful, as well as suggesting opportunities to develop aspects of your own teaching. Most of these introductory sections also contain suggestions for further reading that will support your exploration of thinking skills through the activities in *Thinking by Numbers*.

Teaching children to think for themselves is at the heart of primary education. It is all too easy to focus on the demands of the curriculum and its assessment and forget that the facts and knowledge have to be connected with an understanding of this curriculum content to help the learner make sense of it all. Without this understanding learners cannot use the information they have been taught and see how it relates to other ideas or knowledge that they have already. At the core of the thinking skills movement in education is the belief that this kind of thinking is teachable. This belief has been inspired by the work of two leading educators.

History of thinking skills

In Israel after the Second World War, many refugee children had been through traumatic early experiences. On traditional tests, such as IQ tests or standardized tests of achievement, many of these children scored so badly that they seemed 'unteachable'. Working to integrate such children Reuven Feuerstein refused to accept this conclusion and devised ways to find out exactly which kinds of thinking they were unable to do, how they could be helped to develop these skills, and, therefore, each individual's *potential* for learning.

Feuerstein developed a set of techniques and tasks called 'instruments' that helped these learners succeed on subsequent tests. These methods were termed 'dynamic', in the sense that children were studying the process of learning and the change that took place. Feuerstein argued that such a process was much more likely to predict how a person might then learn in the future. Many of Feuerstein's ideas have influenced work on teaching thinking skills, in particular his emphasis on the importance of the interaction of the teacher, or 'mediation' of thinking.

Another important figure in thinking skills (or 'Critical Thinking', as it is called in the United States), is the American philosopher Matthew Lipman. As a university professor, he thought that his students had been encouraged to learn facts and to accept opinions, but not to think for themselves. He developed a programme, therefore, called 'Philosophy for Children', which aims to help younger people (from six-year-olds to teenagers) to think by raising questions about stories that they read together. The teacher uses children's natural curiosity about the stories in order to promote active participation and learning. One of Lipman's basic convictions is that children are natural philosophers, and that they view the world around them with curiosity and wonder, which can be used as a basis for thinking and reasoning.

Both Feuerstein and Lipman, though from very different starting-points, hold a similar belief in children's abilities. They have demonstrated that through thinking exercises and activities learners can exceed the predictions of achievement which tests may have suggested is their limit of competence. This, then, forms the basis of techniques in thinking skills – realizing children's potential. Their work has inspired many others to explore and develop approaches which help children to become more effective learners as they start to think for themselves. The aim of this book is to help you, as a teacher, to see how this kind of thinking can be developed.

Teaching thinking

Some people argue that the idea of trying to teach general thinking skills is misguided because in practice thinking always occurs in a specific situation. Further, they believe that it is better to concentrate on teaching subjects and developing specific and detailed knowledge. However, *Thinking by Numbers* has been developed on the principle that there are common features of thinking in different situations, that it is helpful to try to apply techniques learned previously in new situations. For example, once you have used a graphic organizer, such as a Venn diagram, to compare and contrast themes in traditional tales in literacy, you can use the same technique to compare and contrast in other curriculum areas, such as family life in different eras in history.

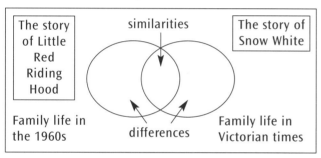

Since 1999, the national curricula for England and Wales now specifically include thinking skills (see page 6 for more details). In Scotland the *5–14 Guidelines* emphasize the capacity for independent thought through enquiry, problem solving, information handling and reasoning, as well as identifying learning and thinking skills in the core skills and capabilities. So the current challenge for teachers is not whether to teach thinking skills, but how best to teach them!

Approaches to teaching thinking skills

There is a host of different programmes and approaches which advocate teaching thinking. These can be categorized broadly into whether they adopt an 'enrichment' approach where they are taught through extra or separate lessons, or an 'infusion' approach where the particular skills are taught through the normal lessons that schools provide. There are certain advantages and disadvantages to adopting these two different teaching approaches. If thinking skills are taught separately it is possible to make skills and techniques explicit, but there is a danger that they may not be used, except in special 'thinking' lessons. However, if they are taught as part of other lessons, such as mathematics or history, there is also a danger that the skills and techniques will become submerged by the curriculum content and not be seen as skills that can be applied elsewhere.

We believe that it is necessary to do both – to have a mixture of 'thinking lessons' with discussion of the kinds of thinking that are involved, and 'subject lessons' where skills can be applied and developed, but perhaps less explicitly. Identifying some lessons as 'thinking maths' lessons gives a clear signal to the children that you are looking for something different in the way that they work and the way they talk and listen. It is challenging to make the time to develop speculation or reasoning in every lesson, but it is also difficult to make sure it happens at *some* time in *some* lessons. We suggest that the activities in the different units can be used as a way to emphasize aspects of thinking that you wish to develop. You may then choose to develop other similar lessons where you can re-use the structure of the activities, or use some of the ideas and techniques in other subject areas.

> ### Suggestions for further reading
> H. Sharron and M. Coulter, *Changing Children's Minds: Feuerstein's Revolution in the teaching of Intelligence* (Birmingham, Questions Publishing Company, 1994)
>
> M. Lipman, *Thinking in Education* (Cambridge University Press, 2003)
>
> C. McGuinness, *From thinking skills to thinking classrooms: A review and evaluation of approaches for developing pupils' thinking* [DfEE Research Report RR115] (Norwich, HMSO, 1999)
>
> V. Wilson, *Can Thinking Skills Be Taught? A paper for discussion* (Edinburgh, Scottish Council for Research in Education, 2000) [Available at: http://www.scre.ac.uk/scot-research/thinking/index.html]

Thinking skills and the National Curriculum

Classifying thinking skills

There are more ways to think about thinking than you could imagine! Amongst the wealth of lists, frameworks, models and taxonomies of thinking that have been developed, many people have heard of the 'Bloom's Taxonomy', which is considered the original way of classifying 'higher order thinking'. This taxonomy is basically a three-tier model:

- **knowledge** – in the form of facts, concepts, rules or skills
- **basic thinking** – relatively simple ways of understanding, elaborating and using what is known
- **higher order thinking** – a learning process which leads to a deeper understanding of the nature, justification, implications and value of what is known.

The National Curriculum in England uses five classification headings to denote thinking skills that should be embedded across all subject areas so pupils learn how to learn. These are:

- evaluation
- creativity
- enquiry
- reasoning
- information processing.

However, no single classification or framework can ever fully describe the complexity of all the kinds of thinking we experience. What is missing in both the original version of Bloom's work and in the National Curriculum list is the role of the thinker in thinking – one's own awareness, reflection and engagement. This metacognitive component (i.e. thinking about how we think) is an essential ingredient in developing a learner's understanding of their own thinking and the ability to think for oneself. The following table shows how *Thinking by Numbers* works alongside these thinking classifications to develop thinking skills.

Bloom's Taxonomy	National Curriculum	Thinking by Numbers	
Knowledge Abstracts and universals Using specifics Knowledge of specifics	*Information processing*	**Unit 1: Sort it out!**	*Unit 6: Think on!*
Basic thinking Application Comprehension			
Higher order thinking Evaluation Synthesis Analysis	*Reasoning* *Enquiry* *Creativity* *Evaluation*	**Unit 2: That's because …** **Unit 3: Detective work** **Unit 4: What if?** **Unit 5: In my opinion**	

Comparison of Bloom's Taxonomy, the National Curriculum and *Thinking by Numbers*

The National Curriculum

The National Curriculum categories contain the following breakdown of skills, which form the basis for the units in the *Thinking by Numbers* series.

Information processing skills

These enable pupils to locate and collect relevant information, to sort, classify, sequence, compare and contrast, and to analyse part/whole relationships.

Reasoning skills

These enable pupils to give reasons for opinions and actions, to draw inferences and make deductions, to use precise language to explain what they think, and to make judgements and decisions informed by reasons or evidence.

Enquiry skills

These enable pupils to ask relevant questions, to pose and define problems, to plan what to do and how to research, to predict outcomes and anticipate consequences, and to test conclusions and improve ideas.

Creative thinking skills

These enable pupils to generate and extend ideas, to suggest hypotheses, to apply imagination, and to look for alternative innovative outcomes.

Evaluation skills

These enable pupils to evaluate information, to judge the value of what they read, hear and do, to develop criteria for judging the value of their own and others' work or ideas, and to have confidence in their judgements.

The first five units of the *Thinking by Numbers* books are based on these classifications. We have also added two further components:

- ◗ a final unit which provides opportunities for **using and applying thinking skills** covered in the earlier units
- ◗ a **metacognitive skills** element running throughout all of the activities, which aims to develop children's awareness and understanding of the thinking they are doing.

Suggestions for further reading
L.W. Anderson and D.R. Krathwohl (eds.), *A Taxonomy for Learning, Teaching and Assessing: A revision of Bloom's Taxonomy of Educational Objectives* (New York, Longman, 2001)

S. Higgins, J. Miller, D. Moseley and J. Elliot, 'Taxonomy Heaven', *Teaching Thinking, 12*, (Autumn 2003)

Thinking skills in mathematics

Mathematics is an area of the curriculum which is full of opportunities to develop pupils' thinking skills and reasoning abilities. An emphasis on developing strategies, identifying patterns and rules, and clarifying concepts helps children learn mathematics by making aspects of it more explicit in the classroom. Developing reasoning, problem solving and enquiry skills through mathematics can support the development of these 'higher order' thinking skills more widely, and encourage successful learning in other subjects. A number of principles underpin the activities in each of the six units in *Thinking by Numbers*. These will help pupils to see the connections between the way that they have worked on a mathematics task and then how they can apply these skills in other contexts, either in other areas of mathematics or other areas of learning and understanding.

Challenge

Thinking activities must provide a level of challenge. This means that they should not be too easy to complete, nor so hard that the pupils cannot recognize that they have been successful. Alternatively, the activities may have more than one solution, or route to a solution, that can be evaluated by the pupils to decide which is the best answer or approach. Mathematics is a subject which people often think they just 'can't do'. Successfully completing challenges encourages pupils to see that maths is a subject that they can learn to be good at.

Active discussion

Thinking activities need to be talked about. Mathematics has both a vocabulary and a language of its own. Familiar words are used in unfamiliar ways, such as 'product' or 'difference', and it has its own terminology, such as 'numerator' or 'perpendicular'. Pupils will need time to practise speaking mathematically and explain what they are thinking using this language. This can be difficult to do with the whole class, so some paired or small group work is essential to provide opportunities to explore ideas and allow pupils to develop confidence with the vocabulary.

Feedback

Giving feedback will be key in ensuring pupils make progress in a thinking activity. One of the easiest ways to do this is to have 'mini-plenaries' as the lesson develops. Stop the class for a few minutes and ask a group to explain where they are up to. This will give you the chance to highlight successful ways of working, as well as asking for reasons and challenging their thinking.

Review

When developing thinking skills it is important to review both the **content** of the activity and the **process** that the pupils have used to complete the activity. This means talking about the mathematics involved in the task and the way that they have worked (the skills used in collaborating, working systematically, or identifying patterns and rules). It is often helpful to discuss the latter the next time pupils undertake a similar task so that you can remind them of what was successful. A combination of 'mini-plenaries' throughout the lesson, a review at the end of a lesson, then recapping at the beginning of the next lesson will help ensure children understand that you want them to think not just about *what* they have learned, but *how* they have learned it.

Professional development

We advocate that you try out the *Thinking by Numbers* activities as part of your professional development programme. A critical perspective on the lesson is essential. The activities alone will not succeed in developing thinking skills without this perspective. It is helpful to have a colleague with whom to discuss the activities as you try out the different ideas. We believe that a key part of teaching thinking and thinking skills successfully is to have some time and space to reflect on your own teaching so as to increase the emphasis on developing pupils' understanding. The introductory 'brief' and final 'debrief' sections of each activity aim to support this by summarizing the key features of the lessons and indicating aspects for review.

Thinking by Numbers provides a combination of teacher-led activities, then discussion and collaborative working in small groups, followed by some kind of whole class discussion, or plenary, which reviews both the content and process of learning. The results of this approach are usually a higher level of engagement in the activities, more talking and discussion about the activities. The activities themselves are open-ended to the extent that genuine discussion is not only possible but helpful. They are also challenging but enjoyable activities, helping to create a classroom climate where there is an emphasis on succeeding after effort.

As part of this process you should get more opportunities to hear what your pupils think. As you plan these lessons to increase engagement in learning you will need to listen carefully to how your pupils respond. The enjoyment should initially help to sustain more permanent changes in patterns of classroom interaction. The further feedback you get from insights into pupils' understanding will help identify any misunderstanding or misconceptions that you can tackle through 'mediation' or questioning and discussion.

Some suggestions for getting started:

1 **Work with a colleague**. This might be a colleague teaching the same year group, in which case you can investigate the impact of the same activities. Alternatively you may be working with a colleague in another year group, so you might look at similar kinds of activities or similar aspects of thinking. Working with a colleague means you are more likely to keep to your plan, building progress in time for review. Discussing things with someone else helps to clarify our own thinking, and makes it easier to see patterns or themes in what has happened.

2 **Decide what you want to investigate or improve**. It is easier to develop children's thinking if you focus on a particular area that you feel needs improvement. You could:
   - ◗ identify information processing as a key mathematical skill needing improvement
   - ◗ focus on your own questioning and how you probe and challenge your children's thinking
   - ◗ develop more precise use of mathematical language
   - ◗ aim to increase participation in lessons by children who are not usually engaged.

3 **Set a timescale** (at least eight weeks, up to a school year) and plan which activities you are going to use. How often will you have *Thinking by Numbers* lessons? Once a week? Once a fortnight? How will you make sure you have time to review the activities with a colleague?

4 **Try out the activities and review** them as soon afterwards as you can with your colleague. What was different in the lesson compared with other maths lessons? Were you able to see patterns in the children's thinking? Were there any common misconceptions that you needed to tackle? How well did the collaborative tasks go?

5 **Analyse what happened**. If there is improvement, what do you think caused it? The focused practice? Your extra time and effort? The pupils' discussion? Your understanding of their thinking? Would it probably have happened anyway?

6 **Review progress**. What have you learned that you can apply in the longer term? Do some kinds of questions work better than others? Can you use any of the strategies more widely?

How to use *Thinking by Numbers*

The activities in *Thinking by Numbers* can be used in different ways – there is no need to work through them in order, though the final unit is designed to let pupils apply the skills that they have developed. Therefore, for you to assess how well these skills have been learned, it should be used after some of the other activities in the first five units. Some of the activities are based on thinking skills strategies which can be used more widely either in mathematics or other subjects of the curriculum. You should therefore evaluate if there are any aspects of the activity or teaching technique which could be used more generally. Although the books are aimed at different age groups, you may find activities that you can use or adapt in other books in the series. This is particularly true of the generic strategies, such as 'odd one out', which can be used again in mathematics or other areas of the curriculum. See page 24 for a fuller description of some generic activities used throughout the book.

Just as enquiry is at the heart of thinking skills activities for pupils, we believe that it also needs to be a part of the way you use them as a teacher. None of the activities will work by themselves, and they will not all be equally effective since this depends on the existing skills and knowledge of your pupils. You will have to use them critically to see how they can help your pupils' thinking – it is impossible to do this directly, since we cannot see into our pupils' heads and know what they are thinking. Nevertheless, it is possible to plan a series of activities that enable you to find out about pupils' thinking at different times and in different ways. This allows you to infer their level of understanding. Therefore, this needs to be a process of enquiry – finding out what and how your pupils think. The 'Watch out for' and 'Listen for' sections of each activity should help with this process.

The units

The units are based around the classification of thinking skills in the National Curriculum for England and the headings of **information processing**, **reasoning**, **enquiry**, **creative thinking** and **evaluation**. Each unit begins with an overview of these particular aspects of thinking, and ends with a summary looking at how these skills can be developed. Of course, it is not possible to separate the thinking in different activities so that they only involve reasoning or creative thinking. Thinking is a complex activity which involves all kinds of thinking at the same time. It is holistic, multi-dimensional and dependent upon the context that we find ourselves in. The purpose of the tasks in *Thinking by Numbers* is to enable you to focus on a particular kind of thinking and to consider how it can be developed or fostered in your pupils.

Links

The appendices (pages 88 to 95) contain information about how *Thinking by Numbers* relates to the *Framework for Teaching Mathematics* used in England, and the *5–14 Guidelines* for Scotland. A glossary of thinking skills terms is also included on page 96 for reference.

Suggestions for further reading
P. Adey, *The Professional Development of Teachers: Practice and Theory* (Dordrecht, Kluwer Wolters, 2004)

S. Higgins, *Thinking Through Primary Teaching* (Cambridge, Chris Kington Publishing, 2001)

The activities

4 Each activity has a whole class introduction where you will be 'Setting the scene' and modelling the problem to the children.

1 Each activity has an introduction, 'The Brief', and review points, 'The Debrief', to explain the context for the activity. This is the 'professional development' part to help you consider what you want to achieve in the thinking lesson, and later to review how well it achieved its thinking skills aims.

7 Reviewing progress and stimulating further thinking are covered in the 'Moving on' section, as are suggestions to develop the teaching strategy or approach in other mathematics lessons, or in other subjects in 'Where next?'.

Next door numbers

BRIEF

In 'Next door numbers' the children engage in an activity where consecutive numbers are added with the aim of making all the numbers between 1 and 30. As answers are found they are marked on a 1–30 grid. Later answers are sorted into sets to show numbers that can be made by adding two, three, or four consecutive numbers and so on, so that patterns can be found and generalizations made.

Key maths links
- Describe and extend number sequences
- Recognize odd and even numbers to 100
- Recognize simple patterns and relationships

Thinking skills
- Working with patterns and rules
- Organizing information
- Suggest and test hypotheses

Language
number, sequence, pattern, multiple, odd, even, predict, row, column, explain, investigate
What comes next?
Describe the pattern

Resources
PCM 25
PCM 26
1–9 number cards
1–30 number lines

Setting the scene

Use a set of large 1–9 number cards. Give one card each to nine children and ask them to stand facing the class in numerical order. Explain that the order is like next door neighbours in a street. Choose a number and ask who is holding a next door number and what the numbers total. The children identify other consecutive numbers in twos, threes, fours etc. Discuss ways to total strings of numbers, such as the total of three consecutive numbers is the same as three times the middle number. Display a 1–30 grid and explain to the children that they will be adding next door numbers to try and make all the answers on the grid. Suggest they write the additions on the grid.

Getting started

Ask the children to work with a partner and, by adding next door numbers, try to make all the numbers on the grid on PCM 25. Once this has been achieved they sort out the answers made by adding two consecutive numbers and putting them in order. This is repeated with the answers made from three consecutive numbers etc. This will enable the children to identify patterns and sequences, and to predict how these will continue beyond 30. They can use PCM 26 to write their findings.

Simplify
Give each pair of children a set of 1–9 number cards and suggest putting them in order and start by pairs of numbers in sequence, then three etc.

Challenge
Ask the group of children to investigate the effect of adding odd and even numbers and then make generalizations.

Checkpoints

It is important to ensure that both members of the partnership are contributing equally and sharing the work. If a pair is heard to make a generalized comment, such as, *When we add two next door numbers the answer is odd*, ask them to share it with others. Also, watch for children working systematically by working with pairs of numbers first, or who try to make all the answers in order. Share good ideas with the class.

84

 Watch out for ...
Make sure that the children use consecutive numbers all the time and do not choose numbers they know will make an answer on the grid.

Encourage the children to plan how they will work before starting and think about how they will keep track of what they have done.

 Ask ...
- *What do you notice about the answers when three next door numbers are added?*
- *Do you think the answer will be odd or even?*
- *Which answers could be made in more than one way?*
- *What do you think the next answer will be?*

 Listen for ...
Encourage children who begin to see patterns when two, three or more consecutive numbers are added and who begin to generalize about adding odd and even numbers.

Did any children identify a pattern in the numbers they could not make?

Support the children in explaining any of their ideas to a partner.

Moving on ...

Review the number sequences and patterns that the children have found. Ask them to predict the next numbers in the sequences and suggest ways to test their predictions. The children can explain what they have learned about consecutive numbers and how the way they worked might help in other lessons. Ask them to evaluate how well they think they did in the activity.

Where next?
- Find ways to make numbers to 50, 100, and so on.
- Investigate adding consecutive odd or even numbers.
- Play a 'Guess the numbers' game by giving an answer and asking groups to say which two odd numbers have been added.
- Explore ways to add a string of consecutive numbers by adding pairs at opposite ends of the string and working into the centre, for example: $2 + 3 + 4 + 5 = 7 + 7 = 14$.
- Work with doubles and near doubles.

How well did this activity work? Did the children just do the calculations or were they engaging with the activity to discover number patterns and to make simple generalizations in words? Were you surprised by anything some children did or noticed? Did they use any of the strategies from earlier activities?

DEBRIEF

85

---

2 Basic information about mathematical objectives and language are included, along with any resources needed, plus the thinking skills focus.

6 The 'Checkpoints' section gives ideas for how to the keep the activity on track. This section also has suggestions on what to watch and listen out for, and prompts and pointers to stimulate discussion.

5 The 'Getting started' section shows how the activity can be developed through collaborative group work.

3 Each activity has accompanying photocopiable resources. Some are resource sheets for the activities, others aim to support the recording of the activities, particularly by pairs or small groups of pupils (for more information on recording see page 16).

Classroom management

Structure and timing of lessons

Each book in the *Thinking by Numbers* series comprises six units. These are based around the English National Curriculum thinking skills headings of **information processing, reasoning, enquiry, creative thinking** and **evaluation**, with a final unit focused on using and applying the skills acquired through the earlier activities. Each unit contains two activities, with three in the final 'using and applying' unit, giving a total of 13 thinking activities or lessons for each year group. They have been planned as mathematics lessons and cover aspects of the curriculum appropriate for each age group (see the NNS and *Mathematics 5–14* matching charts on pages 90 to 95). You could also use the activities as thinking lessons and follow the suggestions at the end of each unit to develop the ideas and thinking strategies across the curriculum. When planning how to use the activities there are a number of different approaches you could take, and these are outlined here.

Regular thinking skills development

You could work through the activities using a *Thinking by Numbers* activity every two or three weeks. The benefit of this approach is that it provides regular opportunities to highlight the thinking skills you want to develop across the year. In the intervening time you would need to make sure that you refer back to the lessons and activities, as it would be all too easy for your pupils, particularly younger children, to forget what you are looking for in their work in the thinking activities.

Intensive thinking skills development

You could choose to work through the units more intensively, perhaps one activity each week over a term, so that you could then take the skills and ideas further over the course of the year. This may also be more suitable for year groups in England where your teaching is affected by statutory tests, such as Year 6 in particular. A further advantage of this approach is that you can build up some momentum with regular 'thinking maths' lessons. Assuming they go well initially, the children will start to look forward to the lessons and you can then capitalize on this enthusiasm. You will also develop a language around the lessons and activities with your class, and the regular practice will enhance this development.

Integrated thinking skills development

Another possible approach for teachers in England and Scotland is to use the matching charts to the *NNS Framework* or *Mathematics 5–14*. These are provided in the appendices and will enable you to substitute the *Thinking by Numbers* activities where they fit most appropriately in your usual teaching plan. Whilst this is less disruptive to the mathematics curriculum, you will need to work hard to develop the thinking themes in the book. The thinking skills issue here is how you get the children to use what they learn elsewhere. This is always a challenge with any learning at school: how do you get learners to transfer what they know or can do to a new situation? The concept of 'bridging' is a useful one. As a teacher you connect or 'bridge' the knowledge or skills between different contexts. Where you have regular lessons you can mention things that you then refer to in other lessons. The further apart the sessions, the harder you will have to work to make those connections meaningful. *You remember when we used a Venn diagram to look at similarities and differences? Could we do something similar here?*

Managing the lesson

To use the *Thinking by Numbers* activities effectively you will need to think through the method of working. Your pupils will need to have a clear idea of what they are doing, and why, so that in the review sections of the lesson they can evaluate how successful they have been. It is important to get the lessons off to a good start, so the children will need a 'hook' or some initial stimulus to launch into the activity well. This can be either through the way you introduce the activity, the resources that are used, or perhaps the way you make it meaningful to the pupils, tapping into their particular interests or enthusiasms. It is hard to predict exactly how long the different activities will take to complete. Sometimes children become particularly enthusiastic about a particular task and you will struggle to get through everything that is suggested. On other occasions you will have time to review the activities and ask the children to reflect on their learning.

Introducing the lesson

Each activity begins with some kind of whole class introduction or demonstration. In this part of the lesson it is important to explain the activity and its purpose clearly. You should make objectives explicit; explain what you want from the pupils in terms of how they should work and the kind of language they should use. You will need to get feedback from the pupils to evaluate whether they understand what they are doing and know what they will have to do in the next phase of the activity. You may also need to adapt the activities according to the needs of your pupils. Although the activities have been designed for particular ages of pupils, you will need to judge whether some alteration is needed to provide the appropriate level of challenge for your class.

During the lesson

In most of the activities the pupils apply or extend the ideas presented in the introduction by working collaboratively in pairs or small groups. When moving from whole-class to paired or group work, it is useful to discuss or mention how the pairs or groups are going to work together and what you are looking for. At the transition it is worth praising specific behaviours: *I liked the way you sorted out the number cards for your group, David.* Though it is also important to tailor this praise, particularly for older pupils who should be aware of supportive behaviours and active listening strategies: *Your group got started really quickly, Emma, what was it that you each did?* Reinforce the method of sharing ideas, explaining that they can do better together than they can separately, and that copying and ownership of ideas are not factors. The tasks themselves are designed to be challenging and to benefit from some discussion in small groups so that pupils don't just make up their minds quickly. The activities also contain suggestions for differentiation, with advice on simplifications and challenges that should help you to ensure that the level of challenge is maintained as the pupils work through the tasks. Further advice on

the opportunities to develop speaking and listening skills is outlined on pages 18 and 19.

Reviewing the lesson

The hardest part of these activities is in helping pupils to see that particular tactics, strategies or approaches are helpful, without teaching specific solutions or answers. This will require some skilful questioning and discussion. It is important to review both the process that the pupils have used, particularly the collaborative skills of speaking and listening, as well as reviewing the curriculum content and knowledge and understanding of the activities.

It is also a good idea to review some of this as the lesson unfolds, rather than waiting until the end. Whilst the plenary seems to be the logical place to review the lesson, the pupils also know that the lesson is drawing to an end and it can be hard to maintain their interest. Mini-plenaries are, therefore, an essential teaching strategy which can help make the activities successful. These can be very brief, just checking where groups are up to, or sharing a successful technique or tactic being used by some children. *I noticed you've sorted the cards into different groups, can you tell the class how they are organized?* It boosts their confidence if you draw this to the attention of the whole class and gives other pupils who may not be on track a clear hint about what they could do.

Another possibility is to recap at the beginning of the next lesson. This is essential if the *Thinking by Numbers* sessions are a week or more apart. You need to remind the children that these are different lessons which require thinking, explaining, reasoning and evaluating. There should be more time for discussion about what went well previously and what skills or strategies they might find useful. The main aim is to help the pupils understand that they might not be able to see a solution immediately, but by thinking and working together they will be able to complete the activity successfully. In mathematics this is particularly important as it is a subject which pupils tend to think that they are either good at or not good at, rather than a subject that they can all learn to be better at!

Formative assessment and assessment for learning

Formative assessment is about intervening during teaching to improve learning. As a teacher you gather feedback about what is going on (either within a lesson or between lessons) and use that information to alter what you do subsequently. Assessment for learning is a more interactive approach that takes assessment a stage further by involving the learners in understanding what the specific learning objectives are for each activity/ task/lesson so that they can judge how successful they have been in achieving them. This helps teachers and pupils to understand the criteria for being successful at learning, both for short term objectives as well as longer term goals about 'learning to learn' more effectively.

When using assessing for learning it is important to give pupils feedback about what they can do to improve (rather than giving marks or feedback that simply indicates whether they are correct or not). One common technique is to get pupils to give you feedback about how well they think they are doing on an activity or a piece of work. This can be a simple thumbs up/down signal from the class, or getting pupils to use traffic light colours to self-assess a piece of work they have done – green for go ('I understand it and can go on'), orange for getting there ('I could do with a little bit of help'), red for stop ('I'm stuck').

Thinking skills approaches also involve formative assessment. Most of the activities are about giving you, the teacher, information about children's thinking. This lets you assess their understanding and make decisions about how to support the development of that thinking. In addition, pupils are expected to talk about their thinking as they undertake the tasks. Developing this metacognitive talk (talk about their own thinking) is a powerful technique which helps learners understand their learning better.

Furthermore, focusing on what makes for successful learning encourages judgement about that learning and moves the discussion away from the products or outputs (such as a complete page of calculations) to what has been learned (such as, 'I am finding subtraction more difficult than addition'). The concept of transfer is crucial here since it moves learning away from the particular to the more general. *What have you learned today that you can use in the future? What have you learned previously that will help you now?*

Both assessment for learning and thinking skills approaches use collaborative techniques for learning: paired and group work so that learners benefit from discussion with their peers. Both approaches highlight the role of the teacher in effective questioning and discussions with the pupils to move their thinking on. Assessment for learning and thinking skills approaches are clearly complementary. If you are developing formative assessment you will be developing children's thinking skills. If you are developing children's thinking skills and being explicit about the thinking they are doing with them, then this is formative assessment!

Suggestions for further reading

Primary National Strategy, *Excellence and Enjoyment: learning and teaching in the primary years. Planning and assessment for learning: assessment for learning* (Document code: DfES 0521-2004 G) (2004)

Assessment Reform Group, *Assessment for Learning: 10 principles* (London, QCA, 2002) (available online at: http://www.qca.org.uk/ages3-14/ downloads/afl_principles.pdf)

P. Black, C. Harrison, C. Lee, B. Marshall and D. William, *Assessment for Learning. Putting it into practice.* (Maidenhead, Open University Press, 2003)

S. Clarke, *Unlocking Formative Assessment: Practical strategies for enhancing pupils' learning in the primary classroom* (London, Hodder and Stoughton, 2001)

How do you know it is working?

One of the greatest challenges in developing learners' thinking is assessing how well the activities are going. You should feel that the tasks and activities are giving the children opportunities to think and you should get direct and indirect evidence of this. There are a number of ways that you can start to gauge the impact of the activities.

Enjoyment

First and foremost the activities should be enjoyable, both for you and your class. It is important that the activities are regarded as fun because this helps the children to develop their confidence to discuss what they think. It encourages the children to offer opinions and ideas without the worry of being 'wrong'. This aspect of the activities is vital to ensure their success. Thinking is hard work, so it needs to be as enjoyable as possible!

Participation

Enjoyment should lead to increased engagement and involvement in the lessons. One of the ways that you can assess this is by keeping track of who participates. Are the contributions coming from those who are usually involved and usually speak in whole class discussions? Can you use the paired or group work to build pupils' confidence in contributing to a whole class discussion? *I thought that your suggestion was a really good one – can you explain it to the class?* Are you getting spontaneous contributions from those you normally have to ask directly?

Language

The next thing to watch for is language that indicates thinking and reasoning. Are the pupils giving reasons? Do they use words like *then, so, because*? Are they being tentative? (*I think … It could be … It might be …*) or speculative (*What if …? How about if we …?*)? You can start the lesson by saying you want to hear particular phrases, and giving suggestions for how they may be used. Then you need to look out for these first when the children are working in pairs or small groups. Then encourage the children to give longer responses in class discussions, ask them for reasons or examples, or to comment on each other's ideas. One of the most effective ways of encouraging this is simply to

wait longer when you ask a question, and wait a little bit longer at the end of the response whilst indicating that you want them to continue. In mathematics you should also see the children using specific vocabulary more precisely; for example, are they getting more accurate in the use of words like *number, numeral* and *digit*? Or terms like *side, corner, edge* and *vertex*? You should also pay attention to the questions that the children ask. If the lessons are successful, the children will be asking questions about the content of the learning (rather than just about what they have to do).

Reflection

If the activities are working the children should know that they have been successful and that they have been thinking hard. They should show growing awareness of this and be able to talk about their thinking. At first this will come out during the activities or just as you finish. It is a good tactic to get them to review and reflect at the beginning of the next *Thinking by Numbers* task; this will help remind them of what is expected in the next task as well as giving you a chance to assess how much they recall from last time!

Transfer

The long term goal of *Thinking by Numbers* is to develop transferable skills. Evidence of this is shown when children start to refer back to thinking skills activities in terms of what they have learned. You should, therefore, begin to notice that they are using and talking about the skills that they are developing in other maths lessons or in other subjects. If this is spontaneous or unprompted you know that they are using the thinking skills for themselves.

Recording

Opportunities for recording are identified in most of the activities. However, there are a number of issues you will need to consider. The activities are about developing thinking and the lesson must focus on this as the most important outcome. Recording can distract from this if the children become concerned with making sure they 'get it right' when they have to write something down. There are two main aspects of recording. The first is the recording of the particular task. Some of the photocopiable resources are explicitly designed for this. For other activities the children will need to think about the best way to record their thinking and their progress through the activity. The activities are often collaborative so you may need to make copies of the completed sheet for all the children in the group.

The second aspect of recording is to support review of the activities. The 'What did you learn today?' photocopiable sheet (see page 17) is designed to help with this. It may not be appropriate to use it for every activity, but it will help you review aspects of the lesson that enable the children to develop an understanding of their thinking and their learning (see *Formative assessment and assessment for learning* on page 14 for more information about developing thinking about learning). This aspect is cumulative and progressive as you will need to encourage the children to think about:

- their learning
- what they did
- what kind of thinking was involved
- how they worked together
- what lessons or skills they have learned that they can use in the future.

When planning how to incorporate recording into a thinking lesson, it is helpful to consider the following principles.

1 Recording should be purposeful
The record should either help with the process of the task or capture aspects of the thinking that it will be helpful to review.

2 Recording should be integral
If keeping track of what they are doing is not part of the task, it becomes an extra burden and less likely to be completed effectively.

3 Recording should be used
If you ask the children to make some notes on their thinking, or to use the 'What did you learn today?' PCM, you need to make use of it in a discussion either in that lesson or as part of setting the scene for the next activity.

4 Recording should be short
The lessons are about thinking and this needs to be the most important part of the lesson. You will not be able to capture everything that happens; you may need to have some kind of record to keep track of what has happened, but keep it as simple as possible.

What did you learn today?

Name _____ Date _____

> ## What did you learn today? _____
> _____
> _____

What kind of thinking did you do today?

	Yes	No
I remembered things that were useful	☐	☐
I organized my ideas	☐	☐
I thought of reasons	☐	☐
I found out something I did not know	☐	☐
I used a rule or a pattern to work something out	☐	☐
I had a new idea	☐	☐
I was methodical	☐	☐

How challenging was it?

Circle one of the choices on the line.

Very easy   Easy   OK   Hard   Very hard

Working with others

	Yes	No
I asked my teacher a question	☐	☐
I asked my partner a question	☐	☐
I asked a question in my group	☐	☐
I shared my ideas	☐	☐
I changed my mind	☐	☐
I was good at listening to my partner	☐	☐

Speaking and listening

Talking, thinking and learning are all closely related. We can remember things that we have heard, but it is only when we can put these ideas into our own words that we know we have learned them effectively. Speaking and listening are therefore, at the heart of any thinking skills work. Listening to your pupils talk is also the best feedback you can get to assess what they are actually learning. It is therefore essential that the lessons and activities have speaking and listening at their core.

Children should be able to explain not just what they are doing, but why, and that their thinking is about the learning they are involved in. This involves speaking, listening and participating effectively in small and large group discussions. This helps them to learn by using new vocabulary (or words they already know more accurately) to express new ideas and new thinking. This process is difficult and requires time and support. Part of the purpose of the group work is to allow this to happen. Children will hear their peers making suggestions and having ideas about the tasks. As they join in and make their own suggestions they will work together to find a solution. This will help children succeed more independently in future tasks. The discussions with the whole class will help them to be more confident in what they are saying and thinking, and will give you opportunities to provide feedback on what you are looking for in thinking lessons. The table on page 19 sets out a progression in speaking, listening and group discussion and interaction across the primary age range.

Classroom language

Classroom language is like a dialect of English. It has particular features and implicit rules that are different from language outside of school. The way you take turns, as a pupil, is very different from the way you normally take turns in conversation, either with your friends or at home. The teacher's use of questions, in particular, is strikingly different. Questions are often heavily loaded. For example, if you ask 'Why did you write that?', a child may assume that you are challenging them because it is incorrect and that they should have put something else. In a thinking skills lesson you may be wanting them to explain the reasons for their choices, or the decisions they made about what to write down, so as to provide a model for the rest of the class. If a teacher asks 'What do you *think* you should do?', the pupils may assume that you are reprimanding them for not listening, rather than asking them to speculate. It is therefore very important to think carefully about the questions that you ask to try to ensure that your pupils understand you really *do* want to know what they are thinking! Some examples of good questions are provided on page 21.

Talking maths

Mathematical language is also different from everyday English. It is important that children do not just learn and remember the vocabulary, but learn how to use the language to communicate. This will help them to develop their mathematical thinking. Many words have specialist meanings in maths lessons, such as 'odd' and 'even'. Other words may not be encountered outside of these lessons, for example, 'trapezium' and 'numerator'. The *Thinking by Numbers* activities are a chance for children to speak the language of mathematics, rather than just practise its vocabulary.

Suggestions for further reading
Primary National Strategy, *Speaking, Listening, Learning: Working with children in Key Stages 1 and 2. Professional development materials* (Document code: DfES 0163-2004), (2004)

N. Mercer, *Words and Minds: How We Use Language To Think Together* (London, Routledge, 2000)

S. Higgins, *Parlez-vous mathematics? Enhancing Primary Mathematics Teaching and Learning*, I. Thompson (ed.) (Buckingham, Open University Press, 2003)

A skills progression in ...

	... Speaking	... Listening	... Group discussion and interaction
Y1/2	⬤ Speak clearly and expressively in supportive contexts on a familiar topic. ⬤ Order talk reasonably and pace well when recounting events or actions. ⬤ Talk engagingly to listeners with emphasis and varied intonation. ⬤ Able to use gestures and visual aids to highlight meanings.	⬤ Listen actively following practical consequences, e.g.: – looking at a speaker – asking for repetition if needed. ⬤ Able to clarify and retain information: – by acting on instructions – by rephrasing in collaboration with others – by asking for more specific information.	⬤ Talk purposefully in pairs and small groups. ⬤ Contribute ideas in plenary and whole-class discussions. ⬤ Make and share predictions, take turns, contribute to review of group discussion. ⬤ Review and comment on effectiveness of group discussions.
Y3/4	⬤ Sustain speaking to a range of listeners, explaining reasons, or why something interests them. ⬤ Organize and structure subject matter of their own choice, and pace their talk (including pauses for interaction with listeners) for emphasis and meaning. ⬤ Adapt talk to the needs of the listeners (such as to visitors or more formal contexts), showing awareness of standard English.	⬤ Sustain listening independently and make notes about what different speakers say, identifying the gist, key ideas and links between them. ⬤ Able to comment and respond, evaluating a speaker's contribution, or evaluate quality of information provided. ⬤ Able to concentrate in different contexts, including talk without/by actions and visual aids.	⬤ Sustain different roles in group work (with support from a teacher), including leading and summarizing main reasons for a decision. ⬤ Talk about language needed to carry out such roles and how they contribute to the overall effectiveness of the work. ⬤ Reflect constructively on strengths and weaknesses of group talk.
Y5/6	⬤ Develop ideas in extended turns for a range of purposes. ⬤ Assimilate information from different sources and contrasting points of view, present ideas in ways appropriate to spoken language. ⬤ Use features of standard English appropriately in more formal contexts. ⬤ Make connections and organize thinking.	⬤ Listen actively and selectively for content and tone. ⬤ Able to distinguish different registers, moving between formal and informal language according to the audience, and emphasize or undercut surface meanings. ⬤ Able to discern different threads in an argument or the nuances in talk.	⬤ Organize and manage collaborative tasks over time and in different contexts with minimal supervision. ⬤ Negotiate disagreements and possible solutions, by clarifying the extent of differences, or by putting ideas to the vote. ⬤ Vary the register and precision of their language and comment on the choices made in more formal contexts.

Adapted from Primary National Strategy, *Speaking, Listening, Learning: Working with children in Key Stages 1 and 2 Handbook* (Norwich, DfES/HMSO, 2003)

Collaborative group work

Collaborative group work is an essential part of thinking skills teaching. The opportunity to work with a partner or in a small group is essential. This is where children can explore their own thinking, hear other people's ideas, be tentative, make mistakes, but be supported and encouraged by their peers. This is how an individual develops confidence in new ways of thinking. However, it does not happen automatically. You will need to make time for it, support, nurture and encourage it.

Plan for it

Thinking about who is going to work with whom, and how, is essential. It won't just happen until the class are used to this way of working, and even then there will be new skills they can develop. Most thinking skills lessons are based on mixed groups that are not based on current levels of attainment. However, you will need to monitor who works well with whom and support the children in working with a wider range of their peers.

Make it explicit

The children need to know that they are expected to work together, and that you are expecting them to help each other. This needs continual reinforcement with the whole class in the introduction, mini-plenaries and review sections of lessons (praising and reminding groups and individuals helps, too).

Teach pupils how to work in groups

Not all children find it easy to cooperate. They may well need the first few activities to focus on learning to work together. It is worth making this a part of your learning objectives for speaking and listening (see pages 18 to 19). In one of the early sessions (if you have not done so already), it is worth agreeing class rules for working in groups or a 'working together protocol'. Such an agreement should be phrased positively about what children should do and might include things like:

- Make sure everybody has a turn in speaking
- One person speaks at a time
- Look at the person who is talking (make eye contact)
- Listen actively (positive body language such as nodding or an open posture)
- Speak clearly
- Explain what you mean
- Respond to what other people say
- Make a longer contribution than just one or two words
- Give reasons for what you think
- Make it clear when you disagree that it is with what has been said (with your reasons) and not a person.

However, it is important that the precise wording comes from the children and that the agreement is posted publicly where it will always be visible in the classroom. The children will use it!

Start small

Pairs are the easiest groups to start with. In Key Stage 1 this should be the main aim. Even very young children should be able to cooperate in pairs, particularly if the cooperation is structured in some way (such as taking turns in a game). Moving from pairs to fours is a good tactic too. A paired task can be reviewed by two pairs to reach agreement, then this larger grouping can form the basis for a further activity.

Make sure the tasks require cooperation

Consider strategies such as having one recording sheet, or set of resources that need to be shared, or assign specific tasks to each member of the group. As groups get bigger you may need to assign different roles and let the children practise the different skills required (for example, leader, note taker, summarizer, clarifier). In the beginning it is best to use existing friendships as the basis for organizing the groups, but don't let them get too cosy. Learning to work with people who are not close friends is an important skill for life!

Suggestions for further reading
L. Dawes, N. Mercer and R. Wegerif, *Thinking Together: Activities for teachers and children at Key Stage 2* (Birmingham, Questions Publishing Co., 2000)

Talking points

Getting started

How are you going to tackle this?

What information have you got to help you?

What do you need to find out or do?

How are you going to do it? Why that way?

Can you think of any questions you will need to ask?

What do you think the answer will look like?

Can you make a prediction?

Supporting progress

Can you explain what you have done so far?

What else do you need to do?

Can you think of another way that might have worked?

What do you mean by ...?

What did you notice when ...?

Are you beginning to see a pattern or a rule?

If someone is stuck ...

Can you say what you have to do in your own words?

Can you talk me through where you are up to?

Is there something that you know already that might help you?

How could you sort things out to help you?

Would a picture help, or a table/sketch/diagram/graph?

Have you talked with your partner/another pair/group about what they are doing?

Reviewing learning

What have you learned today?

What would you do differently if you were doing this again?

When could you use this approach/idea again?

What are the key points or ideas that you need to remember?

Did it work out the way you expected?

How did you check it?

Remember – one way to ask a question is just to wait!

Suggestions for further reading
Association of Teachers of Mathematics, *Primary Questions and Prompts* (Derby, ATM, 2004)

Thinking skills across the curriculum

There are a number of general teaching strategies that you can explore to support the activities in *Thinking by Numbers*. They are helpful because you can use the same technique in different contexts and develop thinking across the curriculum. Each time you use these strategies you can focus on the children's thinking that you want to develop. The children become familiar with the techniques and can get straight down to the learning involved. The strategies are also useful in assessing the children's understanding. If you first **demonstrate** a technique or approach, you can then set an activity which the children **undertake** to develop their thinking. This is as far as most approaches to thinking skills go. However, if you then set a challenge where the children have to **generate** their own activity based on what they have done, you will see them reveal their understanding of the thinking required. This cycle of **demonstrate**, **undertake** and **generate** ensures that the thinking becomes embedded.

Odd one out

In this strategy the children are presented with three items and asked to choose one as the 'odd one out' and to give a reason. Items are chosen to ensure that a range of answers is possible. Pupils can also be asked to identify the similar corresponding characteristic of the other two, or features common to all, to develop their vocabulary and understanding. In mathematics this leads naturally on to a discussion of the properties of numbers and to identifying numbers which have a range of properties. It can easily be extended to work on shapes or into other subjects. Selecting three items with different possible reasons is essential. When the children design their own game, it is essential that you emphasize that there should be more than one solution or 'answer'. It leads on to identifying common properties that the odd one out lacks.

9, 5 and 10 – which is the odd one out and why?

9 because it's a square number ... 10 because it has 2 digits or because it is even ... 5 because it is prime ...

Living graphs

The strategy involves a graph or a chart as the basis for an activity where the children have to relate short statements to the more abstract structure of a graph. The use of statements that children can understand easily, but which they then have to discuss and interpret, helps them to make sense of both the representation of the graph and the information it is based on. This works well in mathematics and science, but also in other subjects where quantitative information is used, such as history and geography.

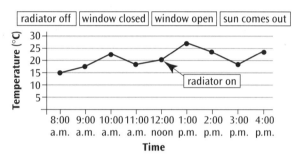

Sorting strategies

Venn diagrams, Carroll diagrams, grids and matrices are effective strategies to display information visually. They support skills such as collecting, sorting, classifying and organizing ideas and information across the curriculum. Sorting techniques are powerful because they provide examples of what a concept or idea is and importantly what it is *not*.

Always, sometimes, never

Another useful strategy is to have a set of statements, such as 'triangles have three sides' or 'multiples of 3 are odd' and ask the children if they are 'always' true, 'sometimes' true or 'never' true. This works well in mathematics and science: in other subjects you may need to set these categories along a continuum to provoke discussion.

As before, asking the children to make up statements that are always, sometimes or never true is a good way to extend the task (and their thinking).

Fermi questions

The approach of Enrico Fermi, who was an Italian scientist who used to pose questions to get his team thinking and working together, works well in the classroom. At school a question such as: *How many balloons would it take to fill the school hall?* requires the children to ask a number of related questions along the lines of, *How big is a balloon? How big is the hall?* This particularly develops estimation and approximation skills. Discussion and reasoning is an important part of the process of answering them. Other questions might be: *How many chocolate beans will it take to fill a litre lemonade bottle? What is the total mass of all the children in the school?* Or *If everyone in school (or the class) lay down in a line from the school gate (or classroom door), head to toe, where would the line end?* Once the children get used to answering questions like this you can ask them to think up their own.

Mysteries

In this strategy children are given information that they use to answer a central question. They work in pairs or small groups to look through short statements on little pieces of paper or card. Then they have to draw inferences and make links between the pieces of information in order to answer the question. The statements contain enough information to require the children to make inferences or identify misleading 'clues'. A mystery can be mathematical (see Year 6 'Birdwatching' page 70), or designed to support evaluation in other subjects such as history or geography.

Why do we remember Guy Fawkes?	
James the First was king of England between 1603 and 1625	Some people wanted to get rid of the king
Some of Guy Fawkes' friends were very angry with the king because of the way he ran the church	When Guy Fawkes was executed people celebrated by lighting bonfires
The king opened Parliament on the afternoon of November 5th 1605	Lots of Guy Fawkes' friends were also arrested. They were all sentenced to death
Guy Fawkes was found in the cellar underneath the Houses of Parliament with 36 barrels of gunpowder	Guy Fawkes was arrested very early in the morning of November 5th 1605

PMI

PMI stands for 'Plus/Minus/Interesting' and is a technique developed by Edward de Bono (as part of his Cognitive Research Trust [CoRT] programme) to get beyond the basic 'pros and cons' approach and the snap decisions that can result from this. When there is a difficult decision or where evaluation is needed, draw up a table headed up 'Plus', 'Minus', and 'Interesting'. In the column underneath the 'Plus' heading, ask the children to write down all the positive points of taking the action. Underneath the 'Minus' heading they write down all the negative points. In the 'Interesting' column they write any further thoughts that strike them. These can be scored across the class to find out how many plus and minus points there are as a method of voting.

Think/Pair/Share

This is a good general technique to get everyone thinking. Instead of getting a response from an individual pupil, ask the whole class to work out the answer, then see if the person next to them agrees, then ask each pair to discuss what they have agreed with another pair. A further variation gets the children to record their thinking before discussing it with a partner: 'Think/Ink/Pair/Share'.

Activities in this book

Unit 1	**Dress the team (pages 26–29)**
Sort it out!	A grid pattern is used to organize an investigation into the number of different team strips that can be made from different colours of tops, shorts and socks.
Information processing skills	**Make new shapes (pages 30–33)**
	Children use a square and two right-angled triangles to make as many new shapes as possible then identify the properties of the new shapes using sorting activities and a range of applicable criteria.
Unit 2	**How tall? (pages 36–39)**
That's because …	An investigation of the approximate number of head measurements equal to height can be used to work out a person's height from a given head measurement. Children then set themselves a similar challenge to draw conclusions about different measurements.
Reasoning skills	**Lots of boxes (pages 40–43)**
	Children work together to investigate the capacity of the boxes to develop an understanding of the relationship between the depth and area of the base. They then apply this thinking to a practical investigation.
Unit 3	**Lines of four (pages 46–49)**
Detective work	Children work collaboratively to find ways to make a line of four answers on a hundred square using three number cards with addition, subtraction and multiplication.
Enquiry skills	**Bananas are best (pages 50–53)**
	Children investigate whether this statement is true and collect information to find out if bananas are the most popular fruit.
Unit 4	**Design a tile (pages 55–59)**
What if …?	Using a template children create different tile patterns by applying simple rules. They investigate the properties of the different tiles that they create and the different designs that can be produced.
Creative thinking skills	**Lots of legs (pages 60–63)**
	Children investigate the way multiples of 2, 3 and 6 can be combined to a total of 24 in a creative story context.
Unit 5	**Make a monster (pages 66–69)**
In my opinion …	Children use interlocking cubes in ten different colours to make a 'monster' with cubes costing different amounts. They make decisions about the different monsters and evaluate their choices.
Evaluation skills	**Up and up (pages 70–73)**
	Children investigate patterns in the addition of numbers written on rows of bricks. They make changes to the numbers and evaluate the impact of those changes in order to make simple generalizations.
Unit 6	**The Summer Fair (pages 76–79)**
Think on!	A 'Living graph' activity (see page 22) where children have to interpret a graph about attendance at a Summer Fair and match statements about what people were doing there.
Using and applying thinking skills	**Start with a square (pages 80–83)**
	Children investigate number sequences practically in order to help them make generalizations.
	Next door numbers (pages 84–87)
	An investigation of the different totals that can be made with consecutive numbers.

Sort it out!

Information processing skills

> **Information processing** – these skills enable pupils to locate and collect relevant information, to sort, classify, sequence, compare, contrast and analyze part/whole relationships. (QCA 2000)

Overview

This unit is about working with mathematical ideas and concepts by gathering information. It is about building understanding by actively working with these concepts and ideas. It is about remembering links and making connections to understand what information is relevant. It is also about working with ideas to develop understanding of their meaning by working with patterns and rules, working with definitions and organizing and representing ideas. It is an essential aspect of mathematical thinking. The activities in this unit are designed to help pupils engage practically with ideas and information so as to build their knowledge and understanding of mathematical concepts.

Strategies

Information processing skills can be broken down further into the following kinds of behaviours or activities that pupils can do:

- ○ **Find relevant information**
  Remember, recall, search, recognize, identify
- ○ **Collect relevant information**
  Retrieve, identify, select, gather, choose
- ○ **Sort**
  Group, include, exclude, list, make a collection or set
- ○ **Classify**
  Sort, order, arrange *by kind or type*
- ○ **Sequence**
  Order, arrange *by quantity/size/weight*, put in an array
- ○ **Compare**
  Find similarities (and differences), examine, relate, liken
- ○ **Contrast**
  Find differences/similarities, examine, distinguish
- ○ **Analyze part/whole relationships**
  Relate, consider, sort out, make links *between parts and wholes* (e.g. component/integral object (such as the face of a cube); member/collection; portion/mass; stuff/object; place/area; feature/activity; especially in terms of fractions, ratios and the like).

Questions

Can you think of something that might help? What does this remind you of?
Give me an example of a ... Is ... an example? Can you give a counter-example?
What would come next? What would come before this?
Why is it the same/different? What makes it a ...? What is it like? What makes a ... different from a ...?

Dress the team

BRIEF

In 'Dress the team' a school team has been given some shirts, shorts and socks in red, blue and yellow. There is insufficient of each colour for the whole team to be dressed the same. The rule is made that every player must be dressed differently. Using a 3 × 3 grid and sorting labels the children find ways to organize the different outfits. The activity is intended to encourage classification and organization as the children find all the solutions and arrange the outcomes into a sorting grid.

Key maths links

- Sorting by one or two criteria
- Organizing information
- Explain methods and reasoning

Thinking skills

- Information processing
- Sort and classify
- Compare and contrast
- Explore relationships

Language

sort, set, organize, display, diagram, criteria, problem What is the same/ different?

Resources

PCM 1 (one per pair)
PCM 2 (one per pair)
card pictures (of three colours of shirt, shorts and socks)

Setting the scene

Display large card pictures of each colour of shirt, shorts and socks. Explain that a school has been given these clothes to wear for inter-school games. Each item of clothing comes in red, blue and yellow but there are not enough for everyone to have the same outfit. The school decides that everyone in the team will dress differently and they need to know how many different outfits can be put together. Draw a 3 × 3 grid and write labels for the colours of the shorts across the top and the shirts on the left side.

Getting started

Working in pairs, the children try to find all the possible combinations of the three colours and articles of clothing. There are 27 altogether, but don't tell the children this – challenge them to work it out for themselves. Encourage systematic working by asking them to think and plan first about how they will work.

Simplify

Using the 3 × 3 grid on PCM 1 and the set of shirt and shorts colour labels on PCM 2 the group draw or write the outfits that will go in each rectangle. Two colours of sock can then be added. The children can use the grid to make labels for a second grid that shows 18 different outfits.

Challenge

Give the group labels that combine two criteria for sorting outfits into a 3 × 3 grid. For example, colours of shorts and socks on one axis and shirt colours on the other. Ask them to explain their reasoning when finding all the combinations and if they could suggest how many there might be if another colour of shirt was added.

Checkpoints

Check how the pairs work together and discuss how to find all the different combinations. Look for pairs who work by changing only one property at a time, for example, by finding all the ways to combine the colours of shirts and shorts before adding the sock colours. Where good methods are being used, ask those children to explain them to the class. Stress the importance of thinking logically when working on this type of activity.

Watch out for ...

Try to ensure that pairs share and discuss ways of working.
Encourage the children to start with one outfit and then only change one thing at a time, for example, if they make one outfit with all red items, they only need to change the shirt colour (to blue and then to yellow).

Ask ...

- Can you think of a way to work out if you have found all the different ways to dress the team?
- You have made an outfit with red shirt, red shorts and blue socks. What can you change to make it different?
- What could you do next?

Listen for ...

Good examples of how the children are organizing their work and offering good explanations of thinking methods should be encouraged and shared. Some children may give predictions by saying, *If we do ... then the result will be ... because ....*
For example, *If we find all the different outfits with shirts and shorts we will have to draw them three times to add each different colour of sock.*

Moving on ...

Review how the children worked as well as the outcomes, and discuss their reasons for thinking they found all the solutions. Ask how organizing the outfits into the array helped to make sure all the outfits had been made and how else they could have been sorted. Can the children suggest how to extend or change the activity? See if they can think of other opportunities to use a grid, or an array, to help them organize their thinking. Together, evaluate how the children think they worked. What did they do well and how could they work better another time?

Where next?

- Sort into Venn and Carroll diagrams using the criteria labels.
- Work with sets of items using up to four criteria.
- Find characteristics that are the same/different in collections of flowers, animals, insects etc. Try a branching tree approach here.
- Create similar logic sets using different criteria.
- Make a set of cards with an outfit on each (27 cards). Play the 'One difference' game: cards are shuffled and shared between 2 to 4 players and one is placed face up in the centre, then players take turns to add a card, on either side of this card, with one difference in the outfit.

How well did this activity work in encouraging children to think systematically and to collaborate in finding solutions to the problem? Did it help them to be organized in how they worked or do they need more experience with this type of activity? Was there anything that surprised you in how some children discussed the problem or tackled it?

DEBRIEF

Dress the team

Name _____ Date _____

Place a property label above each column and each row of the grid. Show the outfit that goes in each space on the grid.

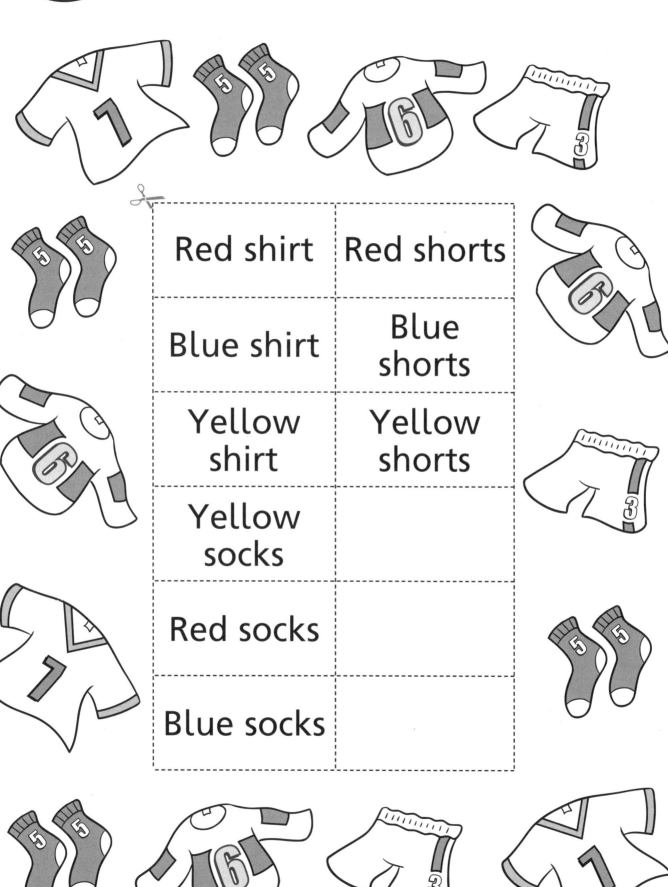

Red shirt	Red shorts
Blue shirt	Blue shorts
Yellow shirt	Yellow shorts
Yellow socks	
Red socks	
Blue socks	

Make new shapes

BRIEF

In 'Make new shapes' the children use a square and two right-angled triangles. Using a given rule the three shapes are combined to make as many new shapes as possible. The properties of the new shapes are identified, including lines of symmetry, and are used for sorting activities using a range of criteria labels. The activity gives valuable experience of working with non-regular shapes and in using the vocabulary of shape.

Key maths links

- Make and describe 2D shapes
- Classify and describe 2D shapes
- Recognize and draw lines of symmetry

Thinking skills

- Sorting and classifying shapes
- Comparing shapes to find similarities and differences

Language

square, triangle, right angle, right-angled, rectangle, pentagon, hexagon, quadrilateral, line of symmetry, mirror line, reflection, equal length

Resources

PCM 3 (one per group/pair)
PCM 4 (one per group/pair)
paper squares (card and/or gummed)
scissors
mirrors
cm-squared paper

 Setting the scene

Display two large squares. Cut one square in half along one diagonal to make two isosceles right-angled triangles. Show how the three shapes can be combined to make a new shape using the rule that only sides of the same length may touch. Make a shape and together make a list of all its properties, such as the name of the shape, the number of sides and angles, sides of equal length, symmetry etc.

 Getting started

Each pair of children needs a number of squares and some squares cut in half to make right-angled triangles. A square and two triangles are combined to make new shapes, drawn on cm-squared paper and cut out. Suggest, before the shapes are drawn, that the children check the shape is not just a reflection or rotation of a shape already made. Groups of children can discuss whether as many shapes as possible have been made. Using the shape property labels (from PCM 4), the children can find different ways to sort the shapes, stick them down and write comments about them on PCM 3.

Simplify

Show the group that instead of moving all three shapes to a new position each time, it is better to put two shapes together and find different positions for the third.

Challenge

Ask the children to design a grid, or a table, to show all of the 3-sided, 4-sided, 5-sided, etc. shapes. See if they can explain why they know that they have found all of the triangles, quadrilaterals etc. Suggest they make new rules for joining the shapes, but not at the corners, so they make shapes with other numbers of sides and find their properties. *Who can make the shape with the most sides?*

 Checkpoints

Encourage the pairs to share their work so they are each finding shapes, doing the sticking and cutting out. Listen to how they approach combining shapes and if there are good methods, such as changing one thing at a time. Stop the class and ask those children to share how they worked. This will help to reinforce the need to work systematically. When the pairs are sorting their shapes, encourage discussion about the properties and make sure that each has a turn to choose the sorting criteria.

Watch out for ...

Check that all the shapes are different and not the same shape in a different orientation.

Ensure that edges of the same length are touching, although new rules can be explored as an extension to the activity.

Ask ...

- ◐ *Are you sure that all your shapes are different?*
- ◐ *Which shapes have you made most of?*
- ◐ *How else do you think you could sort the shapes?*
- ◐ *Explain how you know that shape is a hexagon.*

Listen for ...

Encourage the children to talk about the properties of the shapes as they work and listen for those who can name the shapes, giving their reasons. Some children will compare the shapes with known objects, like houses, and you can ask for the name of the shape. If children are having difficulty in seeing the combined shapes as a single figure, encourage them to draw round it.

Take note of the children who talk about their working methods, such as, *If I put this triangle here it is a quadrilateral but if it goes there it is a triangle.*

 ### Moving on ...

Ask the children to help draw a set of the shapes on the board. Discuss why no more can be made. Review some of the ways that the children used for sorting the sets and how they decided which labels to use. Ask for suggestions about other ways of sorting. How well do the pairs think they worked together? Did they make joint decisions or did one person have all the ideas? What could they improve about working together?

Where next?

- ◐ Sketch or photograph a collection of shapes in the classroom and around the school. Find ways to sort them.
- ◐ Investigate the shapes that can be made by cutting a square into four along the diagonals.
- ◐ Sort the shapes using Venn and Carroll diagrams.
- ◐ Investigate tangrams and other shape puzzles.

Did the children think of strategies for finding different shapes and sorting them or did they tend to work impulsively? Consider to what extent they could recognize shapes as being the same when they were in a different orientation. Did any children surprise you by developing a systematic method for working?

DEBRIEF

Make new shapes

Name _____ Date _____

Choose the labels to go at the top of the columns and use them to sort your new shapes:

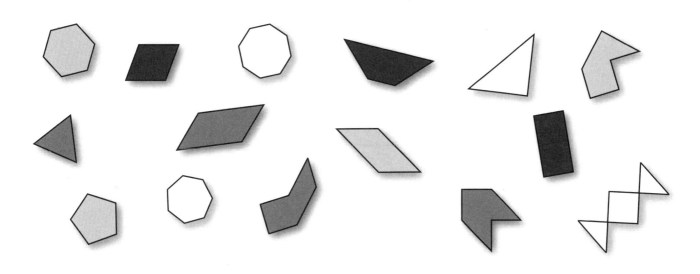

Quadrilateral	All sides equal	Triangle
One right angle	Two sides equal	One line of symmetry
No right angles	No sides equal	Hexagon
Two lines of symmetry	No lines of symmetry	Pentagon
More than one right angle		

Assessing progress

You know that children are developing their skills in information processing when they start to make connections with different mathematical ideas. They should start to show and use this understanding in other lessons. This might be by applying mathematical knowledge in a new situation or it might be in the way that they go about a subsequent task. As their skills in using information develop they should become more precise in the way that they use mathematical language and more systematic in their approach to working and to recording. The techniques that they have used should be developed in other subjects so that their understanding of information processing skills can be transferred to other areas of the curriculum.

Cross-curricular thinking

Literacy

A strategy like 'odd one out' can be used to compare characters from fictional genres, such as different heroines from traditional tales.

Art

The 'odd one out' strategy is also useful for comparing the work of famous artists or to look at similarities and differences in the visual and tactile qualities of materials.

Science

> Little Red Riding Hood, Snow White and Cinderella – who is the odd one out? Why? What makes the other two the same?

Venn diagrams are powerful tools in the teaching of classification. This is particularly valuable in the strands of both variation and classification of living things, and materials and their properties.

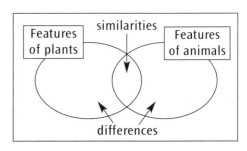

History

Venn diagrams are useful to teach how to compare and contrast in history. Two intersecting sets can be used as a planning tool to identify similarities and differences between different historical periods. Common features go in the intersection and contrasting information on each side.

Geography

The 'odd one out' strategy and Venn diagrams are both helpful in geography. The former can be used to encourage children to use geographical vocabulary as they talk about what makes three different landscapes or features of the environment similar or different. The latter can be used for sorting pictures of buildings or vocabulary related to the character of places. This way, the children will develop an understanding of these concepts by having examples and counter-examples to talk about in a meaningful context.

That's because ...

Reasoning skills

> **Reasoning** – these skills enable pupils to give reasons for opinions and actions, to draw inferences and make deductions, to use precise language to explain what they think and to make judgements and decisions informed by reasons or evidence. (QCA 2000)

Overview

This unit is about reasoning and logical thinking. Reasoning is an essential aspect of mathematics and underpins the development of theorems and proofs through the use of precise definitions and axioms. For pupils of primary age it is important that they have the opportunity to apply their knowledge and understanding of mathematical ideas and concepts logically and systematically as this will enable them to make connections between different concepts and between different areas of mathematics. This will deepen their understanding and develop their confidence as well as helping them see how mathematics can be used as a practical tool in their daily lives.

Developing reasoning skills is also about developing habits of thinking or dispositions as much as it is about specific logical skills. Of course, just because you are good at reasoning does not mean that you are going to be reasonable. Part of thinking reasonably is also dependent upon your knowledge of yourself and the situation in which you find yourself. This metacognitive dimension is essential if you are going to help your pupils become effective thinkers and not just logical.

Strategies

Reasoning skills can be broken down further into the following kinds of behaviours or activities that pupils can do:

- **Give reasons for opinions and actions**
  explain, say because, say why
- **Draw inferences and make deductions**
  see links, make connections, infer, deduce, use words like 'so', 'then', 'must be', 'has to be'
- **Use precise language to explain what they think**
  exemplify, describe, define, characterize
- **Make judgements and decisions informed by reasons or evidence**
  form an opinion, determine, conclude, summarize, *especially where there is more than one course of action or possible solution*

Questions

Explain why ...? Can you give a reason ...? Because ... So ...
Why is ... an example? Is that always/sometimes/never true? What else must be true if ... ? Does it have to be like that? Can you define that? What do they all have in common?
What else is like that? What makes you say that? How can you be sure that ...?

How tall?

BRIEF

'How tall?' is a lively practical investigation where children discover the approximate number of head measurements (circumferences) required to equal height. The children continue by planning what other body measurements they could use instead of the head, e.g. how many hands, feet, full armspans etc. are equal to a person's height. Encourage the children to discuss their thinking and listen to their use of mathematical language as they plan how to work and what equipment to use. Once this problem is solved the children set themselves a similar challenge and from the practical work on the activity they draw conclusions about the measurements.

Key maths links

- Choose and use equipment for measuring length
- Use standard units to measure
- Read scales

Thinking skills

- Give reasons for choices
- Plan how to solve a problem
- Make decisions based on practical activity

Language

ruler, tape measure, height measurer, height, taller, shorter, longer, method, estimate, approximate, approximately, round up or down
How will you work it out?
Guess how many?

Resources

PCM 5 (two per pair)
PCM 6 (one per pair)
tape measures, rulers, height measurers
paper (till rolls/long strips etc.)
hat (≈ 75 cm in circumference) – optional

 Setting the scene

Ask the question, *How do you think you can find a person's height from the size of their head?* If a large hat is available show this asking what the owner's approximate height might be. Give a clue, if necessary, by asking about how many times round someone's head is the same as their height. Discuss the best units to use for the measurements. Write up any estimates before pairs start planning how to answer the problem. Explain that they will work to the nearest whole head measurement.

Getting started

In pairs the children use PCM 5 to write a plan of what they are trying to find out, how they will work, the equipment needed and the units they will use. As the children work stop the activity and share some of the ideas they are using with the class. Again, once the children start to discover that there are about three whole head measurements (circumferences) in their height, discuss their findings and ask them to plan what to find out next on a second copy of PCM 5. Use PCM 6 to generate ideas.

Simplify

The children use long strips of paper to measure their heights by lying down. Show the importance of marking the start and finish of the height. The strips are then measured. Head circumferences can also be found using strips. The children find the number of strips equal to their heights.

Challenge

Suggest the children find their heights and head circumferences then calculate, using mental methods, the number of head circumferences equal to their height, to the nearest whole circumference. This same method is used for all other problems they set themselves.

Checkpoints

It is important for children to plan first how they intend to solve their problem. Observe pairs, as they work, for evidence of good cooperation and listening to each other's ideas. Make it clear to the class that this is a way of working that you are looking for, as well as a solution to the problem. Ask the children to share what they are doing and what they have found out as the work progresses. If you see examples of careful measurement bring them to the attention of the class.

Watch out for ...

Make sure that the children measure as accurately as possible, where necessary, and know how to use the equipment properly.

Check that the children are working to the nearest whole head measurement, handspan etc.

Ask ...

- ❍ *Can you explain what you have done so far?*
- ❍ *About how many handspans tall do you think you are?*
- ❍ *If a person's head measurement is 54 cm about how tall will they be?*
- ❍ *What will you find out next?*

Listen for ...

By talking to other pairs and comparing head circumferences and heights, children may quickly find that they all have a ratio of approximately 3 to 1 when the results are rounded to the nearest whole circumference. Similarly they may find the ratios of other measurements are about the same for everyone. Watch for reasoning language such as *because, then* and *so*.

 ### Moving on ...

Discuss whether each pair has found out similar things about head and height measurements. You may like to use a table or a grid to record the different measurements to help the children with their reasoning. Give an imaginary head circumference and ask the children to work out the person's height. Review what the children decided to do next and what they found. Ask them how working with a partner helped during this activity and what else they shared besides the practical measuring.

Where next?

- ❍ In a larger group compare handspans and feet, or handspans and wrist, measurements.
- ❍ Find out if it is true that a person's full armspan is the same as their height. Compare data from the whole class in a table and see what conclusions the children can draw.
- ❍ Compare birth height with present height. Who, in the class, has grown the most?

For the practical part of this activity it is essential that the children work together for greater accuracy. Reflect on how successful this was, but also consider the extent to which they discussed their methods and findings. Did the children suggest other things they could find out? Evaluate the use children made of reasoning language, such as, *and then, so* and *because*.

DEBRIEF

Name _____ **Date** _____

Write a plan to answer your question.

We are planning to find out: _____

_____

_____

What we plan to do: _____

_____

_____

_____

The equipment we will use: _____

_____

The units we will use: _____

_____

What we did: _____

_____

_____

_____

_____

_____

_____

_____

_____

_____

What we found out: _____

_____

_____

_____

Thinking by Numbers 3 • **Unit 2: That's because …** • **Reasoning skills**

Name _____ Date _____

Write about all the things you have found out about your height and the measurements of other parts of you.

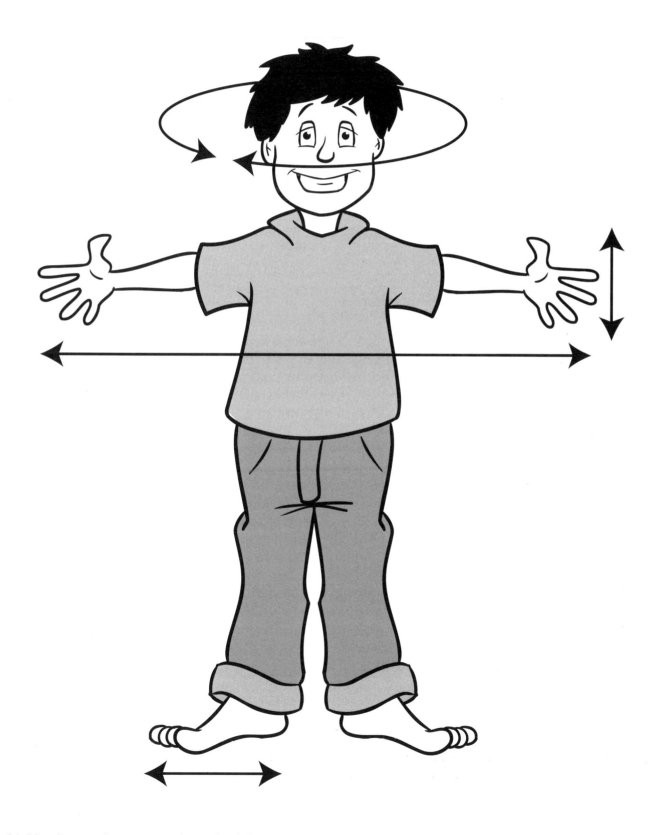

Lots of boxes

BRIEF

In 'Lots of boxes' the children work together to make sets of open boxes from 2 cm-squared paper or card by cutting squares from each corner and folding up the sides. They estimate and then find the capacity of the boxes using 2 cm cubes. The aim of the activity is to develop an understanding of the depth of a container and its importance, as well as the area of the base. This knowledge is used to try and make the largest box from A4 paper.

Key maths links

- Estimate, measure and compare capacity using uniform non-standard units
- Solve problems using capacity

Thinking skills

- Give reasons for opinions
- Explain thinking clearly
- Use evidence to inform thinking

Language

measure, compare, estimate, approximate, approximately, capacity, contains, holds, calculate, cubes
Show your working

Resources

PCM 7 (one per three)
PCM 8 (one per three)
small boxes (different capacity: wide, flat, tall, narrow)
2 cm-squared paper (A4 and 20 × 20 cm)
2 cm interlocking cubes
sticky tape
scissors

Setting the scene

Display some small boxes. Give a box to each table and ask the children to estimate and then find the capacity of their box using 2 cm cubes. Share the results and the accuracy of the estimates with the class. Discuss the best way to fill the boxes with cubes and how the children might work out the number of cubes that will fill the spaces. Explain how to make open boxes from squared paper: by cutting the same sized squares from each corner, folding up the sides and sticking them together. Tell the class that the aim is to find which box will hold the largest number of cubes.

Getting started

Starting with some 20 × 20 cm pieces of 2 cm-squared paper the children work in pairs to make a collection of open boxes. Instructions are given on PCM 7. The capacity of each box is estimated in 2 cm cubes and checked. After commenting on the different capacities on PCM 8 the children are asked to make the largest possible box from a piece of A4 paper using what they have learned from the first part of the activity.

Simplify

Ask the children what strategies they can use for counting the number of cubes, for example, by grouping in tens. Encourage discussion and some explanations about the capacity of the smaller boxes and how this might help them to make the largest box from A4 paper.

Challenge

Encourage the group to find ways of calculating the number of cubes in each box using arrays and other strategies for multiplication.

Checkpoints

It is important to encourage the children to share the task of making boxes and to think about how the printed squares will help with estimation. If any of the children realize how this helps with estimation then ask them to share their thoughts with the class. Encourage reasoning language in their explanations. Before any of the pairs start to make their larger boxes discuss what has been learned about the open boxes and how this might help.

Watch out for …

Try to ensure that pairs discuss strategies for working and share ideas for the estimation and counting of cubes. Make sure they give each other reasons for their thinking behind the strategies. When they are trying to make their largest box discourage them from cutting off squares of any size but prompt them to base their decision on what they found out from making the smaller boxes.

Ask …

- ○ *Why do you think this box holds most/fewest cubes?*
- ○ *If you used a larger piece of paper would it hold more or fewer cubes than the one with four squares cut from the corners?*
- ○ *Why do you think cutting a square that size from each corner will make a box holding the most cubes?*

Listen for …

Look for evidence of children using good strategies for working out the numbers of cubes. Did children count by grouping and, if so, how was this done? Did they use doubling or make arrays for multiplication? Are they using words like *then*, *so* and *because*?

 ## Moving on …

Display examples of the first set of boxes and discuss what was learned. Ask the children for explanations of how this learning helped them to work out the best way to make the largest boxes. *Which size of square cut from the corners gave the largest box and why was this the largest one possible?* Ask the children to review what they have learned about capacity and how they worked together. Can they explain how using what they learned can help with solving problems?

Where next?

- ○ Find the capacity of boxes using metric units.
- ○ Use units of mass to find how much each box will hold using, for example, sand, rice, etc.
- ○ Make different boxes that will hold 24 cubes.
- ○ Estimate and measure the capacity of a collection of bottles of different shapes.

How well did the pairs work together? Did they include reasoning language in their explanations to each other? Think about the extent to which they applied their previous knowledge using reasoning to help solve problems, including the use of counting strategies. Try to evaluate the children's confidence by observing their use of mathematical language.

DEBRIEF

Instructions for making a box

You need: 20 × 20 cm square of paper marked into 2 cm squares
scissors
sticky tape

What you do: Cut out the same size of square from each corner. Fold up the sides and use sticky tape to make an open box.

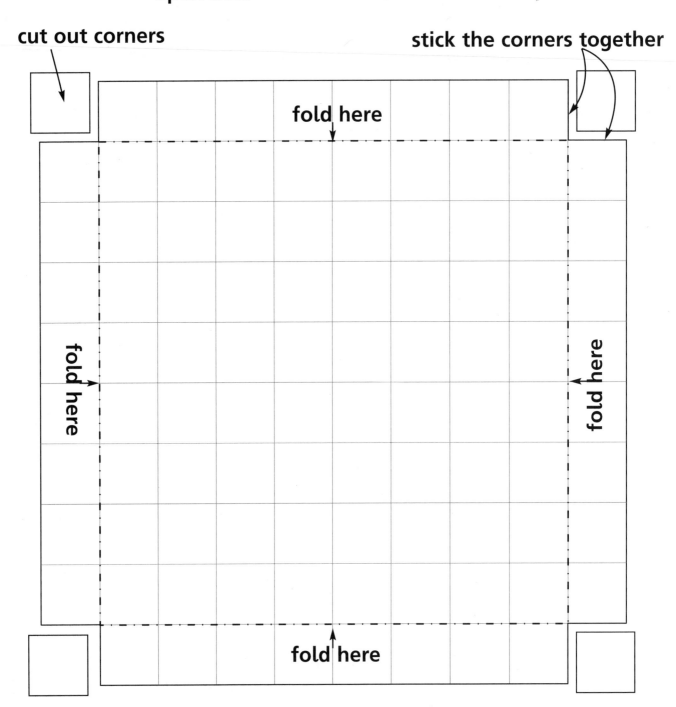

cut out corners

stick the corners together

fold here

fold here

fold here

fold here

In your group plan how to make as many different sized boxes as you can.

Name _____ **Date** _____

Label each of your open boxes with a letter.

Which of your boxes do you think will hold the largest number of 2 cm cubes? _____

Which box will hold the fewest? _____

Estimate the number of cubes you think each box will hold.

_____

Fill the boxes with cubes and count them.

_____

Were you surprised by the results? _____

_____

_____

Give your reasons for thinking this. _____

_____

_____

Now make the largest box you can from a piece of A4 paper.
Explain how you worked and what you found out.

_____

_____

How did finding the capacity of the boxes using cubes help?

_____

_____

Thinking by Numbers 3 • **Unit 2: That's because …** • **Reasoning skills**

Assessing progress

You know that children are developing their reasoning skills when they start using words like 'because', 'then' and 'so' in their discussions and their responses to your questions. They may also start to ask each other 'why?' questions and seek explanations from each other (and from you). Giving reasons as part of explanations then becomes a routine part of thinking lessons. Once you start to ask children why (or to ask another child why a response either was or was not correct) you will be able to assess the reasons in their responses. You need to ensure you ask children to justify correct and incorrect responses, otherwise they will 'read' your question as meaning they have made a mistake if you only ask 'why?' when an answer is wrong. Once children get used to this you can simply wait encouragingly or say 'because ...?' to get them to extend their replies to your questions to assess their reasoning skills.

Cross-curricular thinking

Science

Asking a question such as, *What will happen if?* is a good starting point for scientific reasoning. *What will happen if you put a tea cosy over an icy drink? Will it warm up faster or more slowly? What will happen if you drop a football and a cannonball from the top of a tall building? Will the cannonball reach the ground first?* Using thought provoking questions like these can stimulate scientific reasoning (as well as revealing children's thinking about scientific concepts).

History

A strategy like 'odd one out' can also be used to develop reasoning skills as the children are asked to give reasons for their choice of an 'odd one out' and can be encouraged to distinguish between historical and non-historical reasons. Choose three famous people and ask children to identify an odd one out giving a historical reason.

Literacy

Justifying choices of words and phrases is a good way both to develop reasoning, and to model thinking about composition. Asking a series of questions such as, *Why did you choose that adjective or powerful verb? What others did you consider? Why did you reject those?*, not only gives children the opportunity to give their reasons, but to make them explicit for others to hear.

Geography

Geographical enquiry is supported by reasoning as children express their views about places or changes to the environment. They can use a technique, such as identifying 'Plus, minus and interesting' points to compile a table, then justify the points they have identified with reasons.

Detective work

Enquiry skills

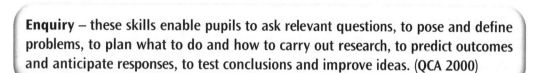

> **Enquiry** – these skills enable pupils to ask relevant questions, to pose and define problems, to plan what to do and how to carry out research, to predict outcomes and anticipate responses, to test conclusions and improve ideas. (QCA 2000)

Overview

Enquiry skills are as much a way of working, or developing particular habits of mind, which keep a range of possibilities open for as long as possible. The process of enquiry is about being flexible, looking for alternatives and testing a range of possible solutions. In mathematics these are essential skills as enquiry develops an understanding of relationships and connections that may not be immediately obvious.

The process of enquiry is at the heart of learning. It is only when you can identify what you need to know, go through a process of finding out and be able to recognize when you have found a solution that you can undertake independent learning. Enquiry skills can, therefore, best be developed in situations where it is not possible to see a solution from the outset and where children will benefit from working together.

There are good opportunities for speaking and listening in presenting the results of an investigation or enquiry. Enquiry lessons are also excellent for review and reflection about the process of learning.

The challenge for the teacher is at the beginning and end of the enquiry process. It is difficult to instruct children in how to ask relevant questions without directing them to a particular investigation or mathematical problem. Similarly, it is difficult enough for pupils to recognize that they have come up with a solution to an investigation, without them realizing that it is a good solution. Identifying what would be a better answer is even more difficult - challenging even for adults! Enquiry skills are also, therefore, about developing more systematic habits of questioning as well as the specific skills in solving a problem.

Strategies

Enquiry skills can be broken down further into the following kinds of behaviours or activities that pupils can do:

- **Ask relevant questions**
  Enquire, be curious, ask, probe, investigate
- **Pose and define problems**
  Frame, propose, suggest, put forward an idea
- **Plan what to do and how to research**
  Think out, plan, sketch, formulate or organize ideas
- **Predict outcomes and anticipate responses**
  Suppose, predict, guess, estimate, approximate, foresee
- **Test conclusions and improve ideas**
  Experiment, test, improve, refine, revise, amend, perfect

Questions

Show me how you could ...? What might work? What ideas have you got? What is a good question to ask? How could you find out? How could you check? Any predictions? What is your best guess? What are you expecting? About how much will it be?

Lines of four

BRIEF

In 'Lines of four' the children work collaboratively in pairs. A set of 0–9 number cards is used to get three numbers which are used with addition, subtraction and multiplication to make an answer between 1 and 49. As the answers are made they are crossed off a grid with the aim of making a line of four answers in any direction. As the children try to make a particular answer it should be possible to listen to their ideas for using the numbers and operations as they discuss alternative solutions. The activity aims to encourage mathematical discussion and flexibility of approach.

Key maths links

- Reasoning about numbers
- Making decisions
- Solving problems using numbers
- Use mental calculation strategies

Thinking skills

- Reasoning
- Making decisions
- Thinking about alternative strategies

Language

add, addition, subtract, subtraction, multiply, multiplication, mental calculation, method, jotting, sign, operation, symbol, equation, horizontal, vertical, diagonal

Resources

PCM 17 (one per pair)
PCM 18 (one per pair)
hundred square

 Setting the scene

Display a hundred square. Shuffle a set of 0–9 number cards and turn over three cards. Write up the three numbers, telling the children that they need to find as many different equations as possible using all three numbers (once in each equation) with the symbols +, –, and ×. Allow a few minutes for the groups to find solutions and then write the equations on the board. Discuss the effect of each operation on the answer and then explain that digits can be combined to make 2-digit numbers. See how many additional equations they can find. Cross the solutions off on the hundred square. Repeat with another three number cards.

 Getting started

Each pair needs the 1–49 number grid on PCM 9 and the set of 0–9 number cards from PCM 10. In turn, the pairs turn over three cards and use them with the operations +, –, and ×, to make one of the numbers on the grid. Once used the cards are returned to the bottom of the pack. This process is repeated until a player has made a straight line of four numbers, horizontally, vertically or diagonally. Encourage the pairs to discuss possible answers and to record the equations they used each time. Suggest that they work out all of the possible equations and see if they can record them systematically.

Simplify

Give the group a 1–30 grid. The three numbers turned over are used with addition and subtraction and each number can be used more than once, if necessary.

Challenge

This group works on a hundred square using division as well as the other mathematical operations, with the aim of getting as many lines of four answers as possible. Ask them to see how few sets of three cards they need to get a line of four.

 Checkpoints

Encourage the children to find solutions together and to discuss how to use their numbers to make a target answer. Highlight good examples of pairs negotiating ways of working by making statements like, *If we do this the answer will be ... and if we do that it will be ...* See if they are being systematic in their use of the three numbers. Look for children who use good mental calculation strategies and then share these with the class.

Watch out for ...

Try to ensure that, as far as possible, the children aim to make answers to get a line of four and that they do not just use the first solution they find with the numbers and operations. What strategies help them?

Ask ...

- ❍ *What happens to your answer if you subtract two instead of multiplying by two?*
- ❍ *What is the highest answer you can make with those three numbers?*
- ❍ *Why do you think you cannot make that answer?*

Listen for ...

Some children may realize that even if they cannot make an answer alongside one or more that have already been found, it is a good strategy to make one nearby.

Applaud children who make use of effective reasoning strategies to make answers larger or smaller by changing the operations.

 Moving on ...

Review some of the different ways that were used to make answers on the grid. Discuss some of the mental strategies the children used and which numbers and operations were easiest or hardest. Ask them how well they think they worked together and how this helped to find solutions. How could they do better another time?

Where next?

- ❍ Turn over two number cards and use them to make a 2-digit target number. Turn over three more numbers and use them with addition, subtraction and multiplication to get the nearest answer possible.
- ❍ Use a computer program which generates a target number, four other numbers and all four operations.
- ❍ Play 'Lines of four' as a game with two pairs aiming to be the first to complete a line.

Consider the extent to which the activity promoted discussion between the working pairs and whether they were flexible enough in their thinking to consider alternative ways of using the numbers and operations to find solutions.

DEBRIEF

Name _____ Date _____

Turn over three cards and use the numbers with any of the operations +, –, and × to make one of the numbers on the grid. Cross the number out.

1	2	3	4	5	6	7
8	9	10	11	12	13	14
15	16	17	18	19	20	21
22	23	24	25	26	27	28
29	30	31	32	33	34	35
36	37	38	39	40	41	42
43	44	45	46	47	48	49

How many lines of four can you make?

Thinking by Numbers 3 • **Unit 3: Detective work** • **Enquiry skills**

0	1	2
3	4	5
6	7	8
	9	

Bananas are best

BRIEF

The statement 'most people like bananas best' is used as the starting point. In groups, the children sort cards to plan the data to be collected and the order of working to enable them to answer the hypothesis. They have the opportunity to discuss what information to collect to find out if bananas are the most popular fruit. As a teacher you will be able to listen to their decisions and how they plan to collect data from the whole class from an organization point of view. Once data has been collected children work in pairs to create a graph and use it to agree or disagree with the hypothesis.

Key maths links

- Test a hypothesis
- Solve a problem by collecting, sorting and organizing information
- Make and interpret a bar chart that represents data

Thinking skills

- Pose and refine a problem
- Plan research
- Predict outcomes
- Redefine the problem

Language

count, tally, vote, frequency table, bar chart, label, axis, axes, most/least popular, favourite
How many more/fewer?

Resources

PCM 11 (one per group of four or six)
PCM 12 (one per pair)
scissors
squared paper
glue

 ## Setting the scene

Write up the statement 'Most people like bananas best'. Ask the class if they think this is true and how it can be tested. Discuss the data needed and how it will be collected efficiently by each group. Write ideas on the board and put them in order.

 ## Getting started

The activity starts with the children working in groups of four or six to order statements on PCM 11 giving stages in the data collection, organization and analysis. Ask them to think about all of the different things they will need to do at each stage. Once they have decided on the data they need, it can be collected from the whole class. Alternatively, they could work in pairs and start the activity before a playtime by collecting data from ten children in the playground. The data from two or three pairs can be combined to make a graph. The children then work in pairs to plan and draw a bar chart. The information from the bar chart is used to answer the hypothesis that 'most people like bananas best'. The children can use PCM 12 to record their findings.

Simplify

This group may need adult support to help order the statements. Alternatively, prompt the order for working to collect the data, and to draw a block graph to complete.

Challenge

The group collects data from another class in addition to their own and draws the bar chart labelled in twos.

 ## Checkpoints

It is important to encourage both the larger groups and the pairs to work and plan together. They need to agree which fruits to use before collecting data, making sure that everyone has the chance to contribute to the discussion. When the pairs are interpreting the graph they need to check they are both involved and coming to the same conclusions.

Watch out for ...

Check that the children are aware of the difference between a block graph and a bar chart where the vertical axis is labelled in ones or twos.

Make sure that both axes are labelled and that the children are aware of the importance of this information.

Ask ...

- ➤ *What do you need to do next?*
- ➤ *How do you know which is the favourite fruit?*
- ➤ *Will the chart be the same if you ask another class?*

Listen for ...

Some children may use the frequency chart to anticipate the graph. Explain that with a small amount of data this may be easy but with larger numbers of people and amounts of data the graph will give a clearer picture.

Encourage the children to compare data on the bar chart rather than merely giving numbers that make a particular choice.

 ## Moving on ...

Review the graphs produced by each group and determine the different fruits that have been chosen. Ask if bananas really are the favourite fruit and if not, which one is preferred. Discuss what other statements could be checked. Review how the larger groups and the pairs worked together. Did they discuss the problems or did someone in the group try to dominate?

Where next?

- ➤ Make a list of other types of foods and use a computer program to input information for graphs of the class's favourite foods.
- ➤ Extend the data to include favourite fruits of, for example, 100 children.
- ➤ Investigate the number of people in the class who eat five portions of fruit and vegetable every day.
- ➤ Ask the children to come up with other questions that they could investigate.

How well did the children work together? Was it a good activity for encouraging a larger group to collaborate on a task or were some children left out? If this was the case consider how the activity could be modified. How well did the task support their enquiry skills? Were they able to answer the question?

DEBRIEF

Cut out the labels. Put them into the order you think you need to work in.

Stick them on paper to remind you what to do next.

See what the bar chart shows about bananas.	Decide which fruits to ask about.
Put labels on the graph.	Make a list of fruit.
Design a sheet to collect the information on.	Draw a bar chart to display this information.
Plan how to collect the information.	Find out information from the graph.

Name _____ Date _____

Use your collected data to make a bar chart on squared paper.

Stick your bar chart here:

Write four things that you can find out from your bar chart.

1 _____

2 _____

3 _____

4 _____

Do you think your bar chart tells you that bananas are the favourite fruit of the people in your class?

_____

Give a reason for your answer.

_____

What question could you ask next?

_____

_____

Thinking by Numbers 3 • Unit 3: Detective work • Enquiry skills

Assessing progress

Evidence that children are making progress in developing enquiry skills can be gained by observing the way that they are working. Enquiry is as much a habit, or an attitude, of keeping a range of possibilities open for as long as possible. Being flexible, looking for alternatives and testing a range of possible solutions are therefore good indications that enquiry skills are developing.

Cross-curricular thinking

Literacy

Another variation on the 'Living graphs' (page 22) strategy is developing the understanding of narratives, both in fiction and non-fiction texts (such as historical narratives), through discussion and enquiry. The graph is replaced with a 'fortune line' about a character's feelings or mood. The children place statements from the narrative on the graph. To do this they need to sequence the text and empathize with the character. Investigating a number of similar narratives (such as traditional tales) will show that they tend to have a similar shaped graph, reflecting the narrative structure and the use of repetition to develop suspense (in *The Three Billy Goats Gruff* and *Little Red Riding Hood*, for example).

History

Fortune lines can also be used in historical enquiry particularly to develop empathy, the statements can either come from real historical figures (the diaries of Samuel Pepys and Anne Frank are good sources) or characters created for the task (such as a child miner in Victorian times).

Science

Developing scientific enquiry means the children must think up questions that can be investigated. An approach called 'Philosophy for children' has been shown to encourage children to develop questioning skills. It uses a stimulus as a starting point, commonly a familiar story, but it can be a poem or a picture, that the children think up questions about. They, then, select one to answer in a class discussion called a 'community of enquiry'. It is possible to extend this into science where questions can be investigated and you can challenge the children to work out how they could find out the answer.

Geography

This approach can work in geography, particularly when a photograph of a stimulating environment or an interesting landscape is used as the starting point. After a discussion of what the children think, their motivation to find out is likely to be enhanced.

Creative thinking – these skills enable pupils to generate and extend ideas, to suggest hypotheses, to apply imagination and to look for alternative, innovative outcomes. (QCA 2000)

Overview

Creative thinking is the kind of thinking that produces new insights, approaches, or perspectives. It is essential in education that learners see that they can come up with new ideas or suggestions which help their own thinking as well as stimulating the thinking of others. No one expects a 7- or 11-year-old to come up with something unique in the history of human development, but unless we value the creativity that young children naturally have they will stop thinking creatively and rely on reproducing ideas they have been given by others.

Creativity is often *not* associated with mathematics in schools, but thinking up new solutions to problems, seeing new connections, or thinking of more efficient or effective alternatives is what mathematicians do. It is not necessary for the ideas to be completely original, just new for the individual pupil or shared with the class for the first time, or it might be that ideas or concepts are seen in a new or unusual way. It is important that pupils feel comfortable in order to be creative. They need to have confidence that their ideas will be accepted and that there is a range of possible answers or solutions to a problem or issue. The aim is to encourage pupils to think up a range of ideas, to have new thoughts or ideas (at least for them) or to extend and develop other people's ideas.

There are a number of techniques and approaches to support creative thinking such as brainstorming, thinking of analogies, visualizing or picturing possibilities. What all these techniques have in common is an emphasis on the flow of ideas. This means that in the early stages of supporting creative thinking it is essential to be uncritical to ensure that thinking is not too restricted.

Strategies

Creative thinking skills can be broken down further into the following kinds of behaviours or activities that pupils can do:

- **Generate and extend ideas**
  Brainstorm, think up, develop, extend
- **Suggest hypotheses**
  Suppose, surmise (*use phrases like 'how about ...?', 'it could be ...'*)
- **Apply imagination**
  Design, devise, visualize, elaborate
- **Look for alternative, innovative outcomes**
  Think laterally, fancy, guestimate, invent

Questions

Can you imagine? What would that look like? How could you change it to make it a ... ? Can you think of a question you could ask? Go on ... What will the answer look like? Another idea? And another ...

Design a tile

In 'Design a tile' the children are presented with rules for creating as many different tiles as possible. The activity provides an opportunity for them to be creative within a mathematical context by deciding on their own rules for producing a tiling design. As the children create the tiles, they need to share ideas and discuss whether designs are the same or different if they are turned through right angles. Also, when they are making their tiling designs they need to agree on the rules.

Key maths links

- Make and describe patterns
- Use and describe turns through right angles
- Understand angles as a measure of turn

Thinking skills

- Develop rules for generating and extending ideas
- Use imaginative ideas for repeating patterns
- Describe ideas

Language

design, pattern, repeating pattern, whole turn, half turn, quarter turn, right angle, describe, explain, investigate, draw, join up

Resources

PCM 13 (one per pair)
PCM 14 (one per pair)
rulers
colouring pencils
squared paper

 Setting the scene

Draw a square on the board with two dots along each side. Explain that it will be used to design a tile using the rules that the dots must be joined by four straight lines, dots along the same side may not be joined, and each dot can only be used once.

With the children's help use the rules to design a tile. Discuss what can be changed to create a new design. Show how two colours can be used so that the same colour only touches at a corner, not along a side. Once most pairs have designed several tiles, stop the activity and share the different tiles the class has created. Choose one design and ask four children to reproduce it on squared paper. Demonstrate how new designs are created by turning the tile. Discuss how to make a rule for repeating the tiles to create a tiling design by turning through one or two right angles.

 Getting started

Each pair needs a copy of PCM 13 to design as many different tile patterns as they can using the rules given. Tell them it is important to discuss how to make each design different and to discuss possible changes. Once several tiles have been designed the pairs choose their favourite and use PCM 14 to investigate different tiling patterns. They can slide or rotate the tile through right angles to the right or left. This part of the activity could be done on a computer.

Simplify

Suggest the children use the resource sheet to draw and colour a number of identical tiles and cut them out. This will enable them to apply their design rule easily and stick the tiles in position.

Challenge

Suggest the children use mathematical language to describe the shapes within their designs and to recognize one or more lines of symmetry. Expect these children to understand that turning a tile through two right angles to the right or left is the same as a half turn.

 Checkpoints

It is important for the pairs to talk about their work and to take care not to repeat designs. Occasionally, stop the class and ask one pair to sketch a design on the board and ask the others if they have found the same one. Talk about the

shapes that can be seen in the design. Where there are instances of good use of mathematical language, share this with the class.

Watch out for ...

Check that the children keep to the initial rules for designing tiles by not using dots more than once and using four straight lines for each one.

Make sure that when the children have decided on their rules for creating tiling designs that they stick to them.

Ask ...

- ❍ *What have you found out?*
- ❍ *Can you explain your rule?*
- ❍ *What will you try next?*
- ❍ *What do you like about that tile?*

Listen for ...

Take note of instances where pairs of children take turns to suggest the rules for their tiling pattern.

Some children may notice that certain tile designs will give the same pattern whichever way they are turned and they will be able to give the reason why.

 Moving on ...

Display some of the tiling patterns and discuss what rule(s) could have been used for each one. Discuss which of the tiles made the most interesting tiling designs and why this was. Ask if working together helped to follow the rules better than working alone and, if so, why. The most creative designs often come from simple patterns and rules.

Where next?

- ❍ Design tiles to use for printing a pattern and devise similar rules to those in this activity.
- ❍ Look for repeating patterns in wrapping paper and describe the rules that were used.
- ❍ Create repeating designs using turtle graphics or a computer art program.
- ❍ Look for designs in the environment and make a book of the patterns around the school.

DEBRIEF

Decide how well the activity worked in helping the children make and keep to rules. By working together were the pairs able to see where designs were the same more easily? To what extent did they talk about their work using mathematical language for following and creating rules? How creative were they? Did any of the tiles produce unexpected results?

Name _____ **Date** _____

Join the dots using four straight lines. Use a dot only once. Dots along the same line cannot be joined.

Colour your designs using two colours. Use the rule that the same colour can only touch at a corner.

Tiling patterns

Name _____ Date _____

Draw and colour the tile design you like best:

Make a tiling pattern. Use the tile you have just drawn.

Describe the rule you have used.

_____

Change the rule and make another tile design:

What is your new rule?

_____

Make two different square tile designs:

Describe the rules you used for these designs.

_____

_____

Lots of legs?

BRIEF

In 'Lots of legs?' the children investigate the way multiples of 2, 3 and 6 can be combined to a total of 24. This is a good number because it has all the other numbers as factors. To make it more creative the activity is set within a scenario of a person keeping pets. It is important to encourage children to plan first, decide how they will work and share the task within their pair so both are fully engaged. Once all the outcomes have been found they need to plan what they will do next.

Key maths links

- Understand the operations of multiplication and division
- Know simple multiplication and division facts
- Solve mathematical problems about numbers

Thinking skills

- Apply imagination
- Find alternative solutions to a problem
- Explain and extend ideas

Language

number, lots of, groups of, multiply, multiplied by, repeated addition, share, twos, fours, sixes, multiple of, answer, problem, divide by, equal subtraction
How did you work it out?
How many?

Resources

PCM 15 (one per pair)
PCM 16 (one per pair)
matchsticks
straws

 Setting the scene

Ask the children what pets they have. Write the type of animal under the labels 2, 4 or 6, depending on the number of legs they have (such as budgie, hamster, stick insect). As most pets will have 4 legs ask what pets could have 2 or 6 legs. Tell a story about a child who receives a surprise present of a huge box with holes in the top. It has labels saying 'THIS WAY UP' and 'HANDLE WITH GREAT CARE'. Inside there are some smaller boxes with different types of small animal. There is a card saying 'Try to work out how many of each animal there are in this box. There are 24 legs altogether'. Ask for suggestions about the animals and how many there could be of each one, e.g. how many birds, how many stick insects etc. Ask for other suggestions.

 Getting started

Before starting the activity pairs of children review the problem and decide how they will work by using the planning sheet PCM 15. They then use PCM 16 to set the scene by writing a simple introduction about someone who keeps different animals with 2, 4 and 6 legs … up to a total of 24. They work out the total number of each pet the person could own. Suggest they devise a simple recording method that does not involve writing out the words.

Simplify

Tell the group to work with a total of 12 legs and suggest they use matchsticks or straws to represent the legs.

Challenge

Suggest the children could include 'pets' with 8 legs, such as spiders. Ask the children to write number sentences to represent the numbers of legs, e.g. $12 \times 2 = 24$, $10 \times 2 + 1 \times 4 = 24$, although they may need to work more simply first. Alternatively, 36 makes a good number to investigate as a harder challenge.

 Checkpoints

As there are a number of solutions it is important to encourage the children to plan how they will work and record solutions. They may decide to share the task, in which case, make sure they confer to avoid duplication. Where there is evidence of the children listening and making suggestions, share these with the class so they are aware of good working methods. Sensible ways of recording and working methodically also need to be shared.

Watch out for ...

It can be common in this type of activity for children to work in a haphazard manner, so suggest they decide on a method where numbers of the different animals are changed systematically.

Make sure that the pairs collaborate and do not try to find solutions without conferring with their partner. Emphasize that they should be thinking up different ideas to talk about with their partner.

Ask ...

- ❍ *What will you change next?*
- ❍ *How many of your answers include pets with six legs?*
- ❍ *Which were the easiest answers to find?*
- ❍ *How could you change the problem?*

Listen for ...

Look out for evidence of children finding patterns in their solutions. If they are working systematically they should notice that if there are six pets with 4 legs, one can be changed to two pets with 2 legs. Look for creative ways for them to do this too, particularly the use of stories about the pets to help them to keep count.

 ## Moving on ...

Begin by sharing some of the plans made at the start and how the pairs might change some things. Share some of the solutions and ask the children why they think there are so many. Ask if there is anything special about 24 (and the 12 used in the simplified activity) and, if so, what it is. Did any children try some other numbers and what did they find out? Review the ways children recorded their answers and how these might be improved.

Where next?

- ❍ Use interlocking cubes to make arrays and find that different arrays can be made for the numbers 1 and 30.
- ❍ Start with 24 matchsticks (or straws) and find how many triangles, squares and hexagons can be made.
- ❍ Investigate other numbers that have 2, 4 and 6 as factors.
- ❍ Develop their creativity by writing up their investigations of the pets as counting poems or number stories to read to younger children.

Ask yourself how well this activity worked in encouraging children to talk and plan how to carry out the task between them. To what extent were they able to suggest ways to extend the investigation together? Think about how the children worked and whether they needed guidance with working logically and creatively.

DEBRIEF

Name _____ **Date** _____

What is the problem?

What are you trying to find out?

How are you going to work together?

How are you going to record what you do?

What will you do first?

How will you continue?

What have you found out?

What will you try next?

Recording 'Lots of legs'

Name _____ **Date** _____

Write an introduction to your activity. Your animals must have 2, 4 or 6 legs each and 24 legs altogether.

Introduction: _____

_____

_____

_____

_____

_____

_____

_____

_____

Work out how many of each animal there could be:

_____

_____

_____

_____

Why do you think 24 gave so many different answers?

_____

_____

_____

_____

Thinking by Numbers 3 • **Unit 4: What if …?** • **Creative thinking skills**

Assessing progress

Assessing the development of creative thinking is challenging as there are often a number of solutions and ideas that can be considered creative in any particular situation. You will have to consider the individual pupil too. A genuinely creative thought for one pupil - something new and insightful for them - may not be so creative in another. Also the process is not necessarily regular or frequent. It is therefore important to consider children's attitudes or their dispositions in different situations. They should be asking questions and be confident to offer ideas. It is this confidence or perhaps playfulness that is the best indicator of creativity, rather than trying to assess specific solutions or outcomes.

Cross-curricular thinking

Literacy

Brainstorming for ideas is a good general technique to develop creative thinking. It is important that it is done in an atmosphere where the children know that offering ideas is more important than coming up with the right answer and where all ideas are accepted uncritically. In literacy this technique can be used when responding to a text to record thoughts and feelings, as well as to stimulate ideas for composition in terms of the content and detail of the vocabulary used. Brainstorming is usually conducted as a whole class activity. It can also be useful to start off in groups so that the children become more independent in using the technique.

Science

Using analogies can be a powerful way to develop scientific understanding in a creative way. Asking children to think of an analogy for something (such as an electric current being like water pipes with the current flowing round a circuit) not only provides an opportunity to compare why they are alike and how they are not alike, but also offers an insight into children's thinking about the science involved.

Design Technology

Coming up with ideas is an essential part of the design process. One technique that can help is to ask children to visualize how the product will be used. Ask them to 'see' it once it is finished: *What will it need to do?, What will make your idea different or special?* This can be the basis for more structured planning and development, though the whole process is a creative one.

Geography

The strategy 'Banned' (where an idea or subject is described without using certain banned words) can easily be developed in other subjects and provides opportunities to develop specific vocabulary. However, it can also be a way to stimulate creative thinking as children will come up with imaginative ways to give clues to words, such as: *It sounds like fountain but starts with an 'm'.* They may find it hard to formulate rules for banned ideas or words. It is usually best to praise their ingenuity and finish with a discussion of creative ways to get round the rules.

In my opinion ...

Evaluation skills

> **Evaluation** – these skills enable pupils to evaluate information, to judge the value of what they read, hear and do, to develop criteria for judging the value of their own and others' work or ideas and to have confidence in their judgements. (QCA 2000)

Overview

Evaluation is about taking responsibility for your own opinions and judgements and being prepared to explain or defend them to others with reasons. It requires confidence in knowing what you think and sensitivity in evaluating or criticizing the work of others. It requires the ability to set and apply criteria to tasks and make judgements based on those criteria. The final stage is presenting these judgements to others and being prepared to defend or change that judgement in the light of feedback. This involves awareness of the feelings of others in giving and receiving feedback – a challenging aspect of effective collaboration and an important aspect of speaking and listening.

In mathematics evaluation is essential in developing confidence in knowing that you have a good solution and understanding why. Mathematics is often perceived as being about applying rules or being able to remember facts and formulas. However, an essential part of being able to think mathematically is to be able to make judgements about which facts to use or which formula to apply. A good solution in mathematics might be an efficient one, or an elegant one, or one that leads to new insights and thinking. Deciding which is the best way to do something mathematically, therefore, often calls for evaluation and judgement.

Strategies

Evaluation skills can be broken down further into the following kinds of behaviours or activities that pupils can do:

- **Evaluate information**
  Appraise, assess, critique, decide
- **Judge the value of what they read, hear and do**
  Review, weigh up, scrutinize
- **Develop criteria for judging the value of their own and others' work or ideas**
  Evaluate, judge, mark
- **Being confident in their judgements**
  Express opinions, disagree, agree (with reasons), resolve

Questions

How could you justify that? What reasons are important? Can you explain ...? How will you check it? Can you argue the opposite? Do you agree? Do you disagree? Which do you think?

Make a monster

In 'Make a monster' the children use interlocking cubes in ten different colours to make a 'monster'. Each colour of cube is priced between 1p and 23p and the children choose cubes to make a 'monster' costing £5. This open-ended activity enables the children to make decisions about adding money to make £5 and to evaluate alternatives. As the children are working you can listen to the decision-making processes as alternative options are discussed. The activity can also highlight the range of strategies children use for adding a series of numbers. You will need a large number of cubes for this activity and may need to borrow extra from another class!

Key maths links

- Making decisions
- Solving problems involving money
- Using mental addition and subtraction strategies

Thinking skills

- Working systematically
- Making and revising decisions
- Information processing

Language

calculate, money, price, cost, buy, spent
How much more/less?
What could you try next?
How did you work it out?

Resources

PCM 17 (one per pair)
PCM 18 (one per pair)
interlocking cubes (in ten colours)
2 cm-squared paper

Setting the scene

Display ten different coloured interlocking cubes and give each colour a price. Explain that cubes need to be chosen for putting into a kit for constructing a 'monster'. Start by saying that cubes must cost no more than £1 and together find ways to make £1. Discuss strategies for adding a string of numbers. These might include doubling and doubling again, or looking for ways of making 10p or 20p etc. Discuss which option will make the most interesting 'monster' and why. Ask what strategies could be used to plan a kit costing £2.

Getting started

Ask the children to work in pairs and, using the price list for cubes on PCM 17 (you may need to adapt this according to the colours you have available), they will plan which cubes to put into a monster-making kit costing exactly £5. Then they can make the monster from the kit and sketch its picture on 2 cm-squared paper, or take a digital photograph of it for the front of a presentation box. When one solution has been found they can plan modifications in a structured way, e.g. exchanging a cube costing 20p for two costing 10p and to evaluate the impact of these changes. Once a pair finds a solution they can use PCM 18 and make a sketch of the monster for another pair to make, give the number of cubes and the cost for each colour.

Simplify

Reduce the number of priced cubes and ask the group to make up a kit that costs less money. Suggest that in their pairs they each choose five cubes and together find the cost of five and then ten cubes. Having done this they can work out how much more they can spend or how the cost needs to be reduced.

Challenge

Suggest the children try to make a monster-making kit that costs £5 using exactly 35 cubes and to think of a good strategy for working out a solution. Ask if there is only one solution.

Checkpoints

Stress the importance of working together to find solutions and remind the children that they should both talk and listen to each other. Give examples of how

66

this might be done. Encourage the children to work systematically by breaking the problem down into smaller chunks. For example, praise those who found how to spend 50p and ask how this could be used in solving further bits of the problem. Occasionally, stop the activity to share good solutions or ways of working with the class. Ask them to evaluate the different monsters that they have created in terms of size and attractiveness or scariness!

Watch out for ...

Keep an eye open for children who work randomly by each taking handfuls of cubes and finding the cost. If this approach is taken, suggest they combine both totals and work out how much more they need to spend and how this can be done. Check that, when adding a string of prices, the children use sensible strategies, such as grouping numbers into multiples of 10 and looking for doubles or near doubles.

Ask ...

- ◗ *Can you show me another way to buy 50p worth of cubes?*
- ◗ *How will you find out how much more you need to spend?*
- ◗ *How can you use what you have done so far to solve a bit more of the problem?*

Listen for ...

Look out for children who are confident with number bonds and quickly identify prices that make multiples of 10p from the price list. Some children will be confident with using multiplication to calculate the cost of multiples of the same colour or group of colours.

 ## Moving on ...

Display some of the models of monsters and discuss which is largest/smallest and why they are different. Hold up a model and ask if fewer cubes could be used by changing lower priced cubes for the equivalent in higher priced ones. Change the question to ask for a larger number of cubes with the same value.

Where next?

- ◗ Find the cost of using three cubes in each colour.
- ◗ Give the exact number of cubes needed for a given amount of money, where there is more than one solution.
- ◗ Use money to find different ways to make £5 to pay for shopping.
- ◗ Choose presents from a price list, up to a given value, for the family.

Did the activity work well or was it too open-ended? How did the children work together and decide about the choice of colours? What did you learn about their understanding and confidence with choosing and using appropriate methods of calculation to solve problems? Were they able to evaluate the different monsters that they devised?

DEBRIEF

Planning for making a monster

Name _____ Date _____

Use the chart to plan how to spend £5 on cubes to make a monster.

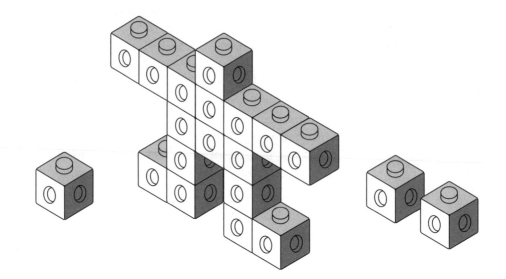

Cube colour	Price per cube	Number of cubes	Total price
orange	5p		
dark blue	10p		
light green	2p		
light blue	23p		
yellow	17p		
black	1p		
red	20p		
dark green	12p		
white	15p		
brown	8p		

Name _____ Date _____

Draw a picture of your monster to show
someone how to make it.

Colour of cubes: _____

_____

Number of each colour: _____

_____

Cost of each colour: _____

_____

_____

_____

_____

Up and up

In 'Up and up' three numbers are written in a row of 'bricks'. Pairs of numbers are added to make the two numbers above and these are added in turn, to make the top number. Different ways of arranging the three numbers are investigated and the numbers at the top compared. The children start with three consecutive numbers at the bottom and then move on to different starting numbers. The activity provides the opportunity for children to investigate number patterns and make simple generalizations.

Key maths links

- ● Solve mathematical problems
- ● Recognize simple patterns
- ● Generalize and suggest extensions

Thinking skills

- ● Reasoning about patterns
- ● Evaluate work by considering alternative solutions
- ● Use judgement about extensions

Language

add, addition, difference, 1-digit number, higher, compare, investigate How many ways? Explain what you did

Resources

PCM 19 (as required)
PCM 20 (as required)

① Setting the scene

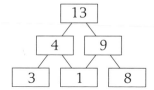

Draw the following diagram on the board:

Ask what has been done. Show how pairs of numbers on the bottom row are added to make the next row, and so on up to the top. Ask how the numbers can be rearranged along the bottom and together find the totals. Rearrange the numbers again and find the new totals. Look for similarities and differences between the answers and decide if another arrangement of the three starting numbers can be found. Explain that you want them to investigate the impact of making changes to the numbers on the bottom row.

② Getting started

Pairs of children work together to complete PCM 19 by choosing three consecutive numbers for the bottom rows and finding all the possible totals for the top rows. Next they try numbers with a difference of 2, then 3 etc. and look for patterns in the top numbers. Ask for suggestions about extending the activity: such as using odd or even numbers, larger numbers or starting with four numbers. Again, emphasize that they should evaluate the impact made by the different starting numbers.

Simplify

Suggest the children use a number line, both to help with selecting the sequences for the starting numbers and for the addition, if necessary.

Challenge

After the group has made some generalizations about the patterns by using number sequences ask if they can find the top number using just the bottom numbers. For example, if the numbers are 4, 5 and 6, these add to 15. Adding the middle number again gives a top total of 20. Ask the group to work with four and then five numbers in the bottom row. Challenge them to identify strategies to find the highest and lowest top numbers, giving reasons based on their earlier work. The children could use PCM 20 to investigate patterns produced by four starting numbers.

③ Checkpoints

Encourage the pairs of children to talk and share ideas about the number patterns, both the ones they choose for the starting numbers and those they find by addition to reach the top. Ask the children to give progress reports as they are working.

Watch out for ...

Some children may not realize that 1, 3, 5 will give the same result as 5, 3, 1 but that 1, 5 and 3 will produce a different result so help them to think about the reason.

Discourage the children from choosing a random set of numbers until they have explored sequences of numbers.

Ask ...

◗ *Why do you think there is a difference of three between the top totals you made with that set of numbers?*
◗ *What other three numbers will give the same difference between the three top totals?*
◗ *What will you try next?*

Listen for ...

Some children might make generalizations about the arrangements of numbers, for example, putting the smallest number in the middle makes the smallest top number.

They should also notice that if the bottom numbers have a difference of 1 the difference between the top numbers in all three arrangements is also 1.

 Moving on ...

Review some of the number sequences the children used and ask them to explain their findings. Discuss how the order of numbers affects the totals and how the activity might be extended. Ask the children to assess how well they worked and shared ideas. What was the best thing about working with someone and what do they need to work on?

Where next?

◗ Find and order all the different top totals possible with the numbers 1–5 at the bottom.
◗ Find how many different 4-digit numbers can be made from four single digits.
◗ Use two counters or coins with a different number on each side. Make as many different 2-digit numbers as possible. Add another counter and find all the different 3-digit numbers ...
◗ Play the 'Highest wins' game. Teams of four players choose three cards from their set of 0–9 number cards and make a 3-digit number. The player making the highest number wins two points.

Consider how well the children worked to share their ideas and how this helped them to find patterns and make general statements about the outcomes. Did they have good suggestions for extending their investigation?

DEBRIEF

Name _____ **Date** _____

1

2

3

4

5

6

7

8

Name _____ **Date** _____

1

2

3

4

5

6

Summary

Assessing progress

The children's increased confidence in their own thinking is one of the hallmarks of improving evaluation skills. It is about taking responsibility for your own opinions and judgements and being prepared to explain or defend them to others with reasons. This requires confidence in knowing what you think. This confidence should be justified, of course, so children should be prepared to change their minds if necessary, in the light of information or reasoning. At this stage it is also important for children to show sensitivity in evaluating or criticizing the work of others.

Cross-curricular thinking

Literacy

Assessment for learning (see page 14) strategies such as 'Traffic lights' are good starting points to develop evaluation skills. You can ask the children to rate a piece of writing that they have done with green for: *I think I can go on*, orange for: *I think I am getting going*, and red for: *I'm at a full stop here*. This opens up the way to discuss criteria for success in the task so that children can evaluate their own work.

Design technology

Evaluation is also central to design technology. The children need to learn to develop evaluation criteria for their designs in order to guide their thinking as they work. This should be an integral part of the process and not simply a retrospective review. Using a digital camera to record the process of designing and making enables the children to recall what they were thinking at the different stages and reflect on the criteria to evaluate the task.

History

A strategy such as a 'Mystery' (see page 23) can help children to use their evaluative skills as they judge the importance of the different 'clues' they have been given. In history this can be a good way to assess understanding of what has been learned in a unit of work as they use their historical knowledge to do this. Clues can easily be written to support a discussion about: *Who was responsible for the Great Fire of London?* for example, to get children to see that the baker may have started the fire, but that there are other factors to consider.

Geography

Some other general techniques that are helpful in developing evaluation skills are those developed by Edward deBono where children are given thinking frames with headings such as 'Plus, minus and interesting' (PMI) (see page 23) or a focus on 'Consider all factors' (CAF). The structure of the sheet helps children to think more carefully and give more considered repsonses. These approaches can be combined with collaborative discussion (such as 'Think, Ink, Pair, Share' where children are asked to consider their responses, make some notes, discuss it with a partner, then in a group) (see page 23). This can be particularly useful in a subject like geography when the children have to evaluate changes to the environment or express their views about people and places.

Think on!

Using and applying thinking skills

> **Using and applying thinking** – in mathematics these skills involve pupils in developing the skills and strategies that will help them solve problems they face both in learning at school and in life more broadly. They involve problem solving in its broadest sense and include the skills of identifying and understanding what the issue or the problem is, planning solutions, monitoring progress in tackling the issue or problem and then reviewing and evaluating any solutions.

Overview

The aim of this unit is to identify some activities for pupils to put their mathematical thinking skills into practice. This will give them the opportunity to evaluate how well they have developed their skills through the earlier activities as well as giving you the opportunity to assess how well they can apply what they have learned. The activities are set as challenges, problems or puzzles.

The process of undertaking these activities relates to the different kinds of thinking in the earlier units. The early stages draw on information processing skills by focusing the children on what they have to do and what they already know. There may be scope for creativity in seeing alternatives or applying knowledge and skills imaginatively to a new problem. Enquiry skills are brought into play during the main part of the activity as any solution is formulated and tested, closely supported by reasoning skills which also help to link the different stages and ensure continuity throughout the process. Evaluation skills are essential to appraise and review any solution and to develop confidence in being successful.

Strategies

Supporting the pupils in using and applying thinking skills to problems is best framed as a series of questions:

- **What do we have to do?**
  What is the problem, challenge or issue to be resolved?
- **Where do we start?**
  What do we know?
  Have we done anything like this before?
  What possibilities are there?
- **How will we know when we have got there?**
  What will a successful solution look like?
- **Are we on track?**
  Is this going to lead us to the answer we imagined?
- **Have we got there?**
  Is this a solution to the problem we were set?
  Could we have done it differently? Is it the best solution?

Questions

What do you have to do? What do you need to know? What do you know already? Have you seen anything like this before? What could you try? Do you think that will work? What will the answer look like? How could you test that? How can you check that? Is this the best answer? How else could you have done it?

The Summer Fair

The 'Summer Fair' activity uses a graph of visitors to a school summer fair. The children have a set of statements relating to the organized activities and they decide where to position them on the 'living graph'. The aim of the activity is to develop the children's understanding of graphs and the information they can convey. It should encourage pairs of children to discuss the statements, listen to each other and make joint decisions. You should be able to listen to these discussions and evaluate their reasoning about decisions.

Key maths links

- Read and interpret a bar chart
- Discuss statements relating to information given in a bar chart
- Sequencing events

Thinking skills

- Interpreting information
- Reasoning and explaining
- Justifying

Language

bar chart, information, explain, label, axis, axes, vertical, horizontal, title, morning, afternoon What time? Put in order

Resources

PCM 21 (one per pair/group)
PCM 22 (one per pair/group)
graph (enlarged copy)
scissors

 Setting the scene

Display an enlarged copy of the graph showing people visiting the Summer Fair at a school. Point to different parts of the graph asking what each means, including the numbers of people shown on the vertical axis and the times on the horizontal axis. Explain that graphs are an important way of showing a lot of information. Offer a statement, *Mr Jones is judging the fancy dress competition*, and discuss what time that is most likely to happen and why. Give other statements, including some that state the time and some which are very open-ended, e.g. *Mrs Jones bought a chocolate cake*. Remind the children about tasks from the earlier units and that they should try to use all the skills they have developed in those activities.

 Getting started

In groups of two or three the children use the graph on PCM 21 and a set of statements on PCM 22. Their aim is to decide, through discussion, where on the graph each of the statements belongs. Remind the children that there are no right and wrong answers and it is quite acceptable to change their minds about positioning a statement.

Simplify

Suggest the group looks for statements in which the time is either given or is fairly easy to judge. Help by asking at what time events in the statements are most likely to have occurred.

Challenge

Provide some blank cards and ask the children to think up their own statements. Suggest they write one statement with an exact answer, another where the time can be worked out using clues from the graph and a third which is open. The children can then try to place each other's statements and give feedback about how difficult or easy the task was.

 Checkpoints

It is essential to encourage the children to talk and listen to each other in their working pairs. Make them aware of the need to explain their thinking to each other about where the statements could be placed. When you hear this happening well, stop the activity and share the explanations with the class, asking if they agree or disagree with their reasons or if there are any alternatives. Encourage them to visualize the Summer Fair as a story that the graph helps to tell.

Watch out for ...

Try to ensure that both partners in a pair are actively involved and that decisions are based on times when events are most likely to occur, for example, that fireworks will most probably be set off when it is dark or as the finale.

Check that the children are aware that times are the important feature of the graph rather than the numbers of people, although these can have a bearing on where statements are placed.

Ask ...

- *Why do you think that statement belongs there?*
- *Can you think of something else that could have happened at that time?*
- *Why are there so few people at the beginning and end of the graph?*

Listen for ...

Some children may start to justify their decisions by stating, *I think it goes there because ...* Share these instances with the class but explain it is also important to ask if their partner agrees and if so, why.

Also, listen out for children who are unsure about placing statements and help them narrow down the choices.

 Moving on ...

Display the enlarged copy of the graph again. Take each statement and ask pairs, in turn, to say where they should go. Give other pairs the opportunity to agree or disagree, giving reasons. Ask what they learned from the lesson that was mathematical. What have they learned about working together and thinking? Suggest giving themselves marks out of ten for how they worked.

Where next?

Ideally the graphs used for this type of activity should be created by the class and linked to other curriculum areas.
- Use statements linked to investigating the local area in geography, such as types of housing.
- In science use graphs about healthy living.
- In PE the graphs can be about running times or distances a ball can be thrown.

How well did the activity work in getting the children to talk, listen and share ideas? Did they give sensible reasons for choosing where to put their statements on the graph? It is important for children to understand that graphs are a means of conveying information concisely. Consider how well this activity helped them to develop this understanding. What thinking skills did the children use? Were they able to draw on any skills developed in the earlier units?

DEBRIEF

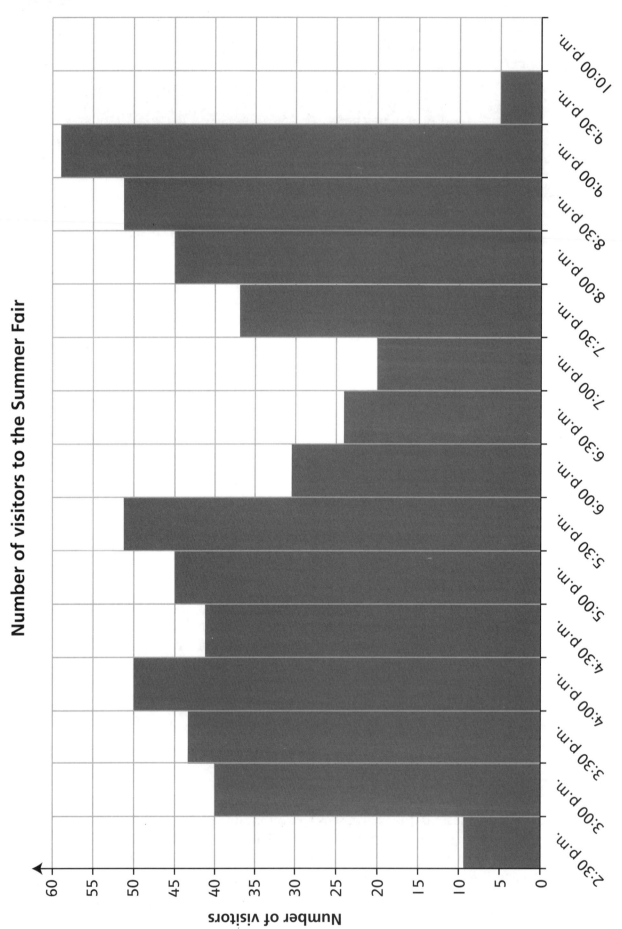

Number of visitors to the Summer Fair

Number of visitors

Time

Mr Singh is given the first prize in the raffle.

Mrs Potter, the headteacher, welcomes everyone to the fair.

The firework display is the most popular event.

Mr and Mrs James bring their three young children to watch the clown.

Aaron wins a teddy bear in the Lucky Dip.

The disco is held after the barbecue.

Some parents arrive early to put cakes and plants on their stalls.

The entries for the children's mini garden are judged.

At 5:30 p.m. the ice-creams are delivered for the barbecue.

People start to go home after the prize giving.

The caretaker locks the school gates.

The tug of war was watched by about 30 people.

Starting with a square

BRIEF

In the activity 'Starting with a square' a sequence of patterns is investigated practically. The sequences start with either one or two squares, and develop into growing letter shapes or bridges. These are investigated and any number patterns generated are used to predict later terms in the sequence. The activity provides the opportunity for children to think about sequences and to discuss ways to predict how the sequences develop through visualization and number patterns. Most children should make simple generalizations.

Key maths links

- Describe and extend number sequences
- Solve mathematical problems and puzzles
- Suggest extensions by asking, *What if ...?*

Thinking skills

- Generate and extend ideas
- Suggest hypotheses
- Compare and evaluate similar mathematical situations

Language

sequence, continue, predict, pattern, relationship, explain, investigate
How many more? Describe the pattern, Describe the rule

Resources

PCM 23 (one per table)
PCM 24 (one per pair)
small squares
interlocking cubes

Setting the scene

Display a square and place 2 squares on the side above and 1 on the side to the right to make an L-shape. Count the number of squares added and then repeat to make a bigger L-shape:

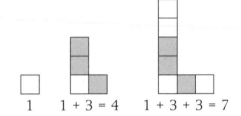

1 1 + 3 = 4 1 + 3 + 3 = 7

Look at the developing sequence and ask the children how many squares will be added to make the next two shapes and what the total numbers will be. Ask for suggestions about the number of squares in the tenth and subsequent shapes. Looking at the second L-shape it will be seen that there are two lots of 3, plus 1 more. Remind them of the earlier units that they have done and see if they can think of any activities that might help them.

Getting started

The children work in pairs and agree which growing shape to use from PCM 23 and how to share the drawing task on PCM 24. The starting shapes are drawn and also, the next three in the sequence. The children write the sequence of numbers in a table. They use the table to predict further numbers, including those that cannot sensibly be drawn and explain their reasoning.

Simplify

Provide small squares (or interlocking cubes) in two different colours to enable the children to work practically for as long as necessary. By working with the growing L-shape they should recognize the sequence of odd numbers and will find it easier to predict later numbers in the sequence.

Challenge

Suggest the children extend their initial sequence by starting with a cube and growing a shape by adding cubes to two or more faces of the starting cube.

Checkpoints

Ensure that the children in pairs are talking and comparing ideas for the development of the sequences and that they both agree about ways to change their initial shape to generate a new number sequence. Listen as the children discuss ideas and ask them to explain their thinking to the class. This is especially important when the pairs are predicting later numbers in the sequence because they will need to visualize the shapes and number patterns rather than work practically.

Watch out for ...

Check that the children see the practical activity as a strategy for generating a number sequence and not just a drawing and colouring exercise. Stress that sketches are acceptable in this situation.

When they are trying to work out later numbers in their sequence some children may forget to add the initial one or two squares.

Encourage pairs to explain why they think certain things are true about their sequence.

Ask ...

- How would the sequence change if you put another square on that edge each time?
- If you put a square on each side of the first one, how would the sequence grow?
- How many squares will there be in your next shape?
- Why do you think that is the answer?

Listen for ...

Some children may say they do not need to draw a growing shape because they have worked out mentally what it will be.

Some children may be able to generalize about their patterns quite quickly by saying that, for example, the tenth shape will have 3×10 squares, plus 1.

Moving on ...

Look at the different number sequences that have been generated. Ask the class to compare the sequences, how they are the same or different, and look at their suggestions for extension. Discuss how working with the squares initially helped them to understand what was happening. Give a sequence starting with a square and ask the children to visualize how many squares must be added around the sides to make a bigger square - and a bigger square.

Where next?

- Investigate sequences that start with a triangle, a hexagon, a cube etc.
- Explore sequences using matchsticks arranged to make a sequence of shapes, e.g. triangles, squares etc.
- Plan a practical way to show a sequence such as 'times three plus two'.

Consider how starting practically helped develop the children's thinking about sequences and their visualization strategies. Were most of the children able to understand and explain about the sequences and could they suggest extension ideas? How did the visualization help? Think about the generalizations they made. Was there evidence that they were using any of the skills from the earlier units?

DEBRIEF

 # Starting with a square

1 Grow an L-shape

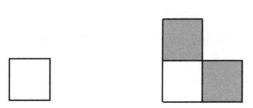 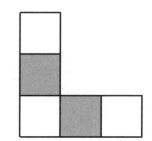

2 Grow a T-shape

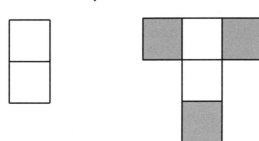 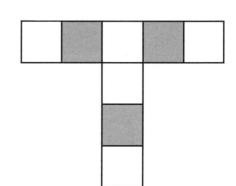

3 Grow a bridge

 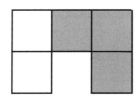 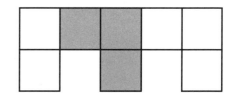

4 Grow an X-shape

 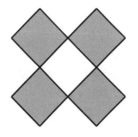 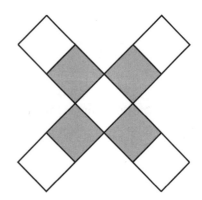

Shapes starting with a square

Name _____ **Date** _____

1 Choose one of the growing shapes from PCM 23.

Copy the first three shapes. Draw the next three shapes in the sequence:

2 Draw a table on the back of this sheet to show the number of squares in the shape and the number of squares you have added to make each new shape.

3 Write as much as you can about the number pattern. _____

_____

Can you predict how many squares
there will be in the 10th shape? _____

How many will there be in the 20th shape? _____

In the 100th shape? _____

Explain how you worked this out. _____

_____

_____

4 Draw how you could change your shape to make a new sequence of numbers. Turn over if you need more space.

Next door numbers

BRIEF

In 'Next door numbers' the children engage in an activity where consecutive numbers are added with the aim of making all the numbers between 1 and 30. As answers are found they are marked on a 1–30 grid. Later answers are sorted into sets to show numbers that can be made by adding two, three, or four consecutive numbers and so on, so that patterns can be found and generalizations made.

Key maths links

- Describe and extend number sequences
- Recognize odd and even numbers to 100
- Recognize simple patterns and relationships

Thinking skills

- Working with patterns and rules
- Organizing information
- Suggest and test hypotheses

Language

number, sequence, pattern, multiple, odd, even, predict, row, column, explain, investigate
What comes next?
Describe the pattern

Resources

PCM 25
PCM 26
1–9 number cards
1–30 number lines

Setting the scene

Use a set of large 1-9 number cards. Give one card each to nine children and ask them to stand facing the class in numerical order. Explain that the order is like next door neighbours in a street. Choose a number and ask who is holding a next door number and what the numbers total. The children identify other consecutive numbers in twos, threes, fours etc. Discuss ways to total strings of numbers, such as the total of three consecutive numbers is the same as three times the middle number. Display a 1-30 grid and explain to the children that they will be adding next door numbers to try and make all the answers on the grid. Suggest they write the additions on the grid.

Getting started

Ask the children to work with a partner and, by adding next door numbers, try to make all the numbers on the grid on PCM 25. Once this has been achieved they sort out the answers made by adding two consecutive numbers and putting them in order. This is repeated with the answers made from three consecutive numbers etc. This will enable the children to identify patterns and sequences, and to predict how these will continue beyond 30. They can use PCM 26 to write their findings.

Simplify

Give each pair of children a set of 1-9 number cards and suggest putting them in order and start by pairs of numbers in sequence, then three etc.

Challenge

Ask the group of children to investigate the effect of adding odd and even numbers and then make generalizations.

Checkpoints

It is important to ensure that both members of the partnership are contributing equally and sharing the work. If a pair is heard to make a generalized comment, such as, *When we add two next door numbers the answer is odd*, ask them to share it with others. Also, watch for children working systematically by working with pairs of numbers first, or who try to make all the answers in order. Share good ideas with the class.

Watch out for ...

Make sure that the children use consecutive numbers all the time and do not choose numbers they know will make an answer on the grid.

Encourage the children to plan how they will work before starting and think about how they will keep track of what they have done.

Ask ...

- ❍ *What do you notice about the answers when three next door numbers are added?*
- ❍ *Do you think the answer will be odd or even?*
- ❍ *Which answers could be made in more than one way?*
- ❍ *What do you think the next answer will be?*

Listen for ...

Encourage children who begin to see patterns when two, three or more consecutive numbers are added and who begin to generalize about adding odd and even numbers.

Did any children identify a pattern in the numbers they could not make?

Support the children in explaining any of their ideas to a partner.

 Moving on ...

Review the number sequences and patterns that the children have found. Ask them to predict the next numbers in the sequences and suggest ways to test their predictions. The children can explain what they have learned about consecutive numbers and how the way they worked might help in other lessons. Ask them to evaluate how well they think they did in the activity.

Where next?

- ❍ Find ways to make numbers to 50, 100, and so on.
- ❍ Investigate adding consecutive odd or even numbers.
- ❍ Play a 'Guess the numbers' game by giving an answer and asking groups to say which two odd numbers have been added.
- ❍ Explore ways to add a string of consecutive numbers by adding pairs at opposite ends of the string and working into the centre, for example:
  $2 + 3 + 4 + 5 = 7 + 7 = 14$.
- ❍ Work with doubles and near doubles.

How well did this activity work? Did the children just do the calculations or were they engaging with the activity to discover number patterns and to make simple generalizations in words? Were you surprised by anything some children did or noticed? Did they use any of the strategies from earlier activities?

DEBRIEF

Name _____ Date _____

Add next door numbers to try and make all the numbers from 1–30.
Write the numbers you added in the box with the answer.

1	2	3	4	5	6
7	8	9	10	11	12
13	14	15	16	17	18
19	20	21	22	23	24
25	26	27	28	29	30

Name _____ Date _____

1 Show how you used two next door numbers to make answers on the grid. Put the numbers in order:

_____

Write what you notice about the number pattern.

_____

_____

2 Show how you used three next door numbers to make answers on the grid. Put the numbers in order:

_____

Write what you notice about the number pattern.

_____

_____

3 Show how you used four next door numbers to make answers on the grid. Put the numbers in order:

_____

Write what you notice about the number pattern.

_____

_____

4 What else did you find out by adding next door numbers?

_____

_____

_____

Assessing progress

The aim of this final unit was to offer some activities for pupils to put their mathematical thinking skills into practice. This should have given you the opportunity to evaluate how well they have developed their skills through the earlier activities as well as the opportunity to assess how well they can apply what they have learned. The grid below is a way for you to review where you think the children have made progress. It is designed for you to use on the whole class, but could be used to reflect on individual children. It is set out as a grid so that you can indicate where you think the first five units were successful, whether the children were able to show these skills in the activities in Unit 6, where you think you have seen progress in other areas of the curriculum, and where you think the children have developed their awareness of their thinking skills. You may wish to review the activities with a colleague who has also been using the *Thinking by Numbers* activities.

Thinking skills		Units 1–5	Unit 6, Using and applying	Across the curriculum	Awareness of the skills
Information processing	locate and collect relevant information				
	sort				
	classify				
	sequence				
	compare and contrast				
	analyse part/whole relationships				
Reasoning	give reasons for opinions and actions				
	draw inferences				
	make deductions				
	use precise language to explain what they think				
	make judgements and decisions informed by reasons or evidence				
Enquiry	ask relevant questions				
	pose and define problems				
	plan what to do and how to research				
	predict outcomes and anticipate consequences				
	test conclusions				
	improve ideas				
Creative thinking	generate and extend ideas				
	suggest hypotheses, to apply imagination				
	look for alternative innovative outcomes				
Evaluation	evaluate information				
	judge the value of what they read, hear and do				
	develop criteria for judging the value of their own and others' work or ideas				
	have confidence in their judgements				

Appendix

Scope and sequence chart

Unit	Unit name	Activity name	Key maths links	Thinking skills	Page no.
1	Sort it out! *Information processing skills*	Dress the team	◐ Sorting by one or two criteria ◐ Organizing information ◐ Explain methods and reasoning	◐ Information processing ◐ Sort and classify. Compare and contrast ◐ Explore relationships	26–29
		Make new shapes	◐ Make and describe 2D shapes ◐ Classify and describe 2D shapes ◐ Recognize and draw lines of symmetry	◐ Sorting and classifying shapes ◐ Comparing shapes to find similarities and differences	30–33
2	That's because … *Reasoning skills*	How tall?	◐ Choose and use equipment for measuring length ◐ Use standard units to measure and solve problems of length ◐ Read scales for measuring length	◐ Give reasons for choices ◐ Plan how to solve a problem ◐ Make decisions based on practical activity	36–39
		Lots of boxes	◐ Estimate, measure and compare capacity using uniform non-standard units ◐ Solve problems using capacity	◐ Give reasons for opinions ◐ Explain thinking clearly ◐ Use evidence to inform thinking	40–43
3	Detective work *Enquiry skills*	Lines of four	◐ Reasoning about numbers ◐ Making decisions ◐ Solving problems using numbers ◐ Use mental calculation strategies	◐ Reasoning ◐ Making decisions ◐ Thinking about alternative strategies	46–49
		Bananas are best	◐ Test a hypothesis ◐ Solve a problem by collecting, sorting and organizing information ◐ Make and interpret a bar chart that represents data	◐ Pose and refine a problem ◐ Plan research ◐ Predict outcomes ◐ Redefine the problem	50–53
4	What if …? *Creative thinking skills*	Design a tile	◐ Make and describe patterns ◐ Use and describe turns through right angles ◐ Understand angles as a measure of turn	◐ Develop rules for generating and extending ideas ◐ Use imaginative ideas for repeating patterns ◐ Describe ideas	56–59
		Lots of legs	◐ Understand the operations of multiplication and division and the associated vocabulary ◐ Know simple multiplication and division facts by heart ◐ Solve mathematical problems about numbers	◐ Apply imagination ◐ Find alternative solutions to a problem ◐ Explain and extend ideas	60–63

Unit	Unit name	Activity name	Key maths links	Thinking skills	Page no.
5	In my opinion … *Evaluation skills*	Make a monster	● Making decisions ● Solving problems involving money ● Using mental addition and subtraction strategies	● Working systematically ● Making and revising decisions ● Information processing	66–69
		Up and up	● Solve mathematical problems ● Recognize simple patterns ● Generalize and suggest extensions	● Reasoning about patterns ● Evaluate work by considering alternative solutions ● Use judgement about extensions	70–73
6	Think on! *Using and applying thinking skills*	The Summer Fair	● Read and interpret a bar chart ● Discuss statements relating to information given in a bar chart ● Sequencing events	● Interpreting information ● Reasoning and explaining ● Justifying	76–79
		Start with a square	● Describe and extend number sequences ● Solve mathematical problems and puzzles ● Suggest extensions by asking, *What if …?*	● Generate and extend ideas ● Suggest hypotheses ● Compare and evaluate similar mathematical situations	80–83
		Next door numbers	● Describe and extend number sequences ● Recognize odd and even numbers to 100 ● Recognize simple patterns and relationships	● Working with patterns and rules ● Organizing information ● Suggest and test hypotheses	84–87

Thinking by Numbers 3 and the NNS Medium-term Plans

The following chart shows how the thinking activities could be used if following the teaching order suggested in the NNS Medium-term Plans. Choose an appropriate activity to suit your class.

Autumn Term

Unit	Unit topic	Thinking by Numbers		
		Activity name	Thinking skill	Page no.
1	Counting, properties of numbers and number sequences	Unit 1: Dress the team	Information processing	26–29
		Unit 4: Lots of legs	Creative thinking	60–63
		Unit 5: Up and up	Evaluation	70–73
		Unit 6: Start with a square	Using and applying	80–83
		Unit 6: Next door numbers	Using and applying	84–87
2–4	Place value and ordering	Unit 6: The Summer Fair	Using and applying	76–79
	Understanding + and –	Unit 3: Lines of four	Enquiry	46–49
	Mental calculation strategies (+ and –)	Unit 5: Make a monster	Evaluation	66–69
		Unit 5: Up and up	Evaluation	70–73
		Unit 6: Start with a square	Using and applying	80–83
		Unit 6: Next door numbers	Using and applying	84–87
	Money and 'real life' problems	Unit 5: Make a monster	Evaluation	66–69
	Making decisions	Unit 1: Dress the team	Information processing	29–29
		Unit 5: Make a monster	Evaluation	66–69
		Unit 6: The Summer Fair	Using and applying	76–79
5–6	Measures, including problems	Unit 2: How tall?	Reasoning	36–39
		Unit 2: Lots of boxes	Reasoning	40–43
		Unit 6: The Summer Fair	Using and applying	76–79
	Shape and space	Unit 2: Make new shapes	Reasoning	30–33
	Reasoning about shapes	Unit 4: Design a tile	Creative thinking	56–59
7	**Assess and review**			
8	Counting, properties of numbers and number sequences	Unit 1: Dress the team	Information processing	26–29
		Unit 4: Lots of legs	Creative thinking	60–63
		Unit 5: Up and up	Evaluation	70–73
		Unit 6: Start with a square	Using and applying	80–83
		Unit 6: Next door numbers	Using and applying	84–87
	Reasoning about numbers	Unit 1: Dress the team	Information processing	29–29
		Unit 3: Lines of four	Enquiry	46–49
		Unit 5: Up and up	Evaluation	70–73
9–11	Place value, ordering, estimating	Unit 2: How tall?	Reasoning	36–39
		Unit 2: Lots of boxes	Reasoning	40–43
		Unit 6: The Summer Fair	Using and applying	76–79
	Understanding + and –	Unit 3: Lines of four	Enquiry	46–49
	Mental calculation strategies (+ and –)	Unit 5: Make a monster	Evaluation	66–69
		Unit 5: Up and up	Evaluation	70–73
		Unit 6: Start with a square	Using and applying	80–83
		Unit 6: Next door numbers	Using and applying	84–87
	Money and 'real life' problems	Unit 5: Make a monster	Evaluation	66–69
	Making decisions, checking results	Unit 1: Dress the team	Information processing	29–29
		Unit 5: Make a monster	Evaluation	66–69
		Unit 6: The Summer Fair	Using and applying	76–79
12–13	Measures, and time, including problems	Unit 2: How tall?	Reasoning	36–39
		Unit 2: Lots of boxes	Reasoning	40–43
		Unit 6: The Summer Fair	Using and applying	76–79
	Handling data	Unit 1: Dress the team	Information processing	29–29
		Unit 3: Bananas are best	Enquiry	50–53
		Unit 6: The Summer Fair	Using and applying	76–79
14	**Assess and review**			

Spring Term

Unit	Unit topic	Thinking by Numbers		
		Activity name	**Thinking skill**	**Page no.**
1	Place value, ordering, estimating, rounding	Unit 2: How tall?	Reasoning	36–39
		Unit 2: Lots of boxes	Reasoning	40–43
		Unit 6: The Summer Fair	Using and applying	76–79
	Reading numbers from scales	Unit 2: How tall	Reasoning	36–39
2–3	Understanding + and −	Unit 3: Lines of four	Enquiry	46–49
	Mental calculation strategies (+ and −)	Unit 5: Make a monster	Evaluation	66–69
		Unit 5: Up and up	Evaluation	70–73
		Unit 6: Start with a square	Using and applying	80–83
		Unit 6: Next door numbers	Using and applying	84–87
	Money and 'real life' problems	Unit 5: Make a monster	Evaluation	66–69
	Making decisions, checking results	Unit 1: Dress the team	Information processing	26–29
		Unit 5: Make a monster	Evaluation	66–69
		Unit 6: The Summer Fair	Using and applying	80–83
		Unit 6: Next door numbers	Using and applying	84–87
4	Shape and space	Unit 2: Make new shapes	Reasoning	30–33
	Reasoning about shapes	Unit 4: Design a tile	Creative thinking	56–59
5–6	Measures and time, including problems	Unit 2: How tall?	Reasoning	36–39
		Unit 2: Lots of boxes	Reasoning	40–43
		Unit 6: The Summer Fair	Using and applying	76–79
7	**Assess and review**			
8	Counting, properties of numbers and number sequences	Unit 1: Dress the team	Information processing	26–29
		Unit 4: Lots of legs	Creative thinking	60–63
		Unit 5: Up and up	Evaluation	70–73
		Unit 6: Start with a square	Using and applying	80–83
		Unit 6: Next door numbers	Using and applying	84–87
	Reasoning about numbers	Unit 1: Dress the team	Information processing	29–29
		Unit 3: Lines of four	Enquiry	46–49
		Unit 5: Up and up	Evaluation	70–73
9	Understanding + and −	Unit 3: Lines of four	Enquiry	46–49
	Mental calculation strategies (+ and −)	Unit 5: Make a monster	Evaluation	66–69
		Unit 5: Up and up	Evaluation	70–73
		Unit 6: Start with a square	Using and applying	80–83
		Unit 6: Next door numbers	Using and applying	84–87
	Understanding × and ÷	Unit 2: Lots of boxes	Reasoning	40–43
		Unit 3: Lines of four	Enquiry	46–49
		Unit 4: Lots of legs	Creative thinking	60–63
10	Mental calculation strategies (× and ÷)	Unit 3: Lines of four	Enquiry	46–49
	Money and 'real life' problems	Unit 5: Make a monster	Evaluation	66–69
	Making decisions, checking results	Unit 1: Dress the team	Information processing	26–29
		Unit 5: Make a monster	Evaluation	66–69
		Unit 6: The Summer Fair	Using and applying	80–83
		Unit 6: Next door numbers	Using and applying	84–87
11	Fractions			
12	Handling data	Unit 1: Dress the team	Information processing	29–29
		Unit 3: Bananas are best	Enquiry	50–53
		Unit 6: The Summer Fair	Using and applying	76–79
13	**Assess and review**			

Unit	Unit topic	Activity name	Thinking skill	Page no.
		Thinking by Numbers		
1	Place value, ordering, estimating, rounding	Unit 2: How tall?	Reasoning	36–39
		Unit 2: Lots of boxes	Reasoning	40–43
		Unit 6: The Summer Fair	Using and applying	76–79
2–3	Understanding + and −	Unit 3: Lines of four	Enquiry	46–49
	Mental calculation strategies (+ and −)	Unit 5: Make a monster	Evaluation	66–69
		Unit 5: Up and up	Evaluation	70–73
		Unit 6: Start with a square	Using and applying	80–83
		Unit 6: Next door numbers	Using and applying	84–87
	Money and 'real life' problems	Unit 5: Make a monster	Evaluation	66–69
	Making decisions, checking results	Unit 1: Dress the team	Information processing	26–29
		Unit 5: Make a monster	Evaluation	66–69
		Unit 6: The Summer Fair	Using and applying	80–83
		Unit 6: Next door numbers	Using and applying	84–87
	Pencil and paper procedures	Unit 5: Make a monster	Evaluation	66–69
		Unit 6: Next door numbers	Using and applying	84–87
4–6	Measures, including problems	Unit 2: How tall?	Reasoning	36–39
		Unit 2: Lots of boxes	Reasoning	40–43
		Unit 6: The Summer Fair	Using and applying	76–79
	Shape and space	Unit 2: Make new shapes	Reasoning	30–33
	Reasoning about shapes	Unit 4: Design a tile	Creative thinking	56–59
7	**Assess and review**			
8	Counting, properties of numbers and number sequences	Unit 1: Dress the team	Information processing	26–29
		Unit 4: Lots of legs	Creative thinking	60–63
		Unit 5: Up and up	Evaluation	70–73
		Unit 6: Start with a square	Using and applying	80–83
		Unit 6: Next door numbers	Using and applying	84–87
	Reasoning about numbers	Unit 1: Dress the team	Information processing	29–29
		Unit 3: Lines of four	Enquiry	46–49
		Unit 5: Up and up	Evaluation	70–73
8	Understanding × and ÷	Unit 2: Lots of boxes	Reasoning	40–43
		Unit 3: Lines of four	Enquiry	46–49
		Unit 4: Lots of legs	Creative thinking	60–63
	Mental calculation strategies (× and ÷)	Unit 3: Lines of four	Enquiry	46–49
	Money and 'real life' problems	Unit 5: Make a monster	Evaluation	66–69
	Making decisions, checking results	Unit 1: Dress the team	Information processing	26–29
		Unit 5: Make a monster	Evaluation	66–69
		Unit 6: The Summer Fair	Using and applying	80–83
		Unit 6: Next door numbers	Using and applying	84–87
11	Fractions			
12	Understanding + and −	Unit 3: Lines of four	Enquiry	46–49
	Mental calculation strategies (+ and −)	Unit 5: Make a monster	Evaluation	66–69
		Unit 5: Up and up	Evaluation	70–73
		Unit 6: Start with a square	Using and applying	80–83
		Unit 6: Next door numbers	Using and applying	84–87
	Pencil and paper procedures	Unit 5: Make a monster	Evaluation	66–69
		Unit 6: Next door numbers	Using and applying	84–87
	Time, including problems	Unit 6: The Summer Fair	Using and applying	80–83
	Making decisions, checking results	Unit 1: Dress the team	Information processing	26–29
		Unit 5: Make a monster	Evaluation	66–69
		Unit 6: The Summer Fair	Using and applying	80–83
		Unit 6: Next door numbers	Using and applying	84–87
13	Organizing and using data	Unit 1: Dress the team	Information processing	29–29
		Unit 3: Bananas are best	Enquiry	50–53
		Unit 6: The Summer Fair	Using and applying	76–79
14	**Assess and review**			

Summer Term

Thinking by Numbers 3 and the NNS Framework

Thinking skill	Unit	Activity name	Counting, properties of numbers and number sequences	Place value and ordering	Estimating and rounding	Fractions	Understanding addition and subtraction	Rapid recall of addition and subtraction facts	Mental calculation strategies (+ and −)	Paper and pencil procedures (+ and −)	Understanding multiplication and division	Rapid recall of multiplication and division facts	Mental calculation strategies (× and ÷)	Checking results of calculations	Making decisions	Reasoning about numbers or shapes	Problems involving 'real life', money and measures	Measures	Shape and space	Organizing and using data
Information processing	1	Dress the team	✓												✓	✓				✓
		Make new shapes														✓			✓	
Reasoning	2	How tall?			✓												✓	✓		
		Lots of boxes			✓						✓						✓	✓		
Enquiry	3	Lines of four	✓				✓		✓		✓		✓			✓				
		Bananas are best																		
Creative thinking	4	Design a tile														✓			✓	✓
		Lots of legs									✓	✓								
Evaluation	5	Make a monster					✓	✓	✓	✓				✓	✓		✓			
		Up and up	✓	✓			✓		✓							✓				
Using and applying thinking skills	6	The Summer Fair	✓												✓		✓			✓
		Start with a square	✓				✓		✓											
		Next door numbers	✓				✓		✓	✓				✓						

94

Thinking by Numbers 3 and the 5–14 Guidelines

Thinking skill	Unit	Activity name	Problem solving and Enquiry	Information Handling	Range and Type of Numbers	Money	Add and Subtract	Multiply and Divide	Round Numbers	Fractions, Percentages and Ratio	Patterns and Sequences	Functions and Equations	Measure and Estimate	Time	Perimeter, Formulae and Scales	Shape, Position and Movement
Information processing	1	Dress the team		✓							✓					
Information processing	1	Make new shapes														✓
Reasoning	2	How tall?	✓										✓			
Reasoning	2	Lots of boxes	✓					✓	✓				✓			
Enquiry	3	Lines of four					✓	✓								
Enquiry	3	Bananas are best														
Creative thinking	4	Design a tile	✓	✓												✓
Creative thinking	4	Lots of legs						✓			✓					
Evaluation	5	Make a monster	✓			✓	✓									
Evaluation	5	Up and up	✓		✓		✓							✓		
Using and applying thinking skills	6	The Summer Fair	✓	✓	✓						✓					
Using and applying thinking skills	6	Start with a square					✓				✓					
Using and applying thinking skills	6	Next door numbers					✓				✓					

Number, Money and Measurement comprises the strands: Range and Type of Numbers, Money, Add and Subtract, Multiply and Divide, Round Numbers, Fractions, Percentages and Ratio, Patterns and Sequences, Functions and Equations, Measure and Estimate, Time, Perimeter, Formulae and Scales.

Glossary

algorithm a step by step procedure that, if followed exactly, will always yield a correct solution to a type of problem

assessment for learning an approach to **formative assessment** where the learner is encouraged to take responsibility for evaluating their own achievement of learning objectives. An aspect of **self-regulation**.

Bloom's Taxonomy a widely used instructional objectives model developed by the prominent educator Benjamin Bloom and colleagues in the 1950s. It categorizes the cognitive, affective and conative domains and includes a systematic list of thinking skills, in categories and sub-categories such as comprehension, application, analysis, synthesis, and evaluation. The last three are considered **higher-order** thinking skills.

brain-based learning a range of techniques and approaches to teaching and learning which take their inspiration from research into how the brain works to identify implications for teaching

brainstorm a technique for rapid production of ideas without critical examination, evaluation or elaboration

bridging a teaching strategy where explicit links are drawn from what has been learned to other related contexts to help **transfer**

cognition the mental operations involved in thinking; the biological/neurological processes of the brain that facilitate thought. Sometimes contrasted with affect or emotion and conation (wanting or willing).

Community of Enquiry the process of developing knowledge and understanding by participating in purposeful dialogue or collaborative discussion. Also the teaching technique used in Philosophy for Children with a class of pupils.

concrete preparation an introductory phase in some teaching thinking approaches where new words are introduced and learners become familiar with what the task is about

constructivism a view of learning in which learners are seen as building or developing their own understanding of how the world works from their experience and interaction with people around them

creative thinking producing new ideas or thoughts. Imaginative thinking that is aimed at producing outcomes that involve synthesis of ideas or lateral thinking; thinking that is not analytical or deductive, sometimes referred to as divergent thinking.

critical thinking a generic term for thinking skills used in the United States. The process of determining the authenticity, accuracy, or value of something; characterized by the ability to seek reasons and alternatives, perceive the complete situation, and change one's view based on evidence and reasoning. Sometimes also called analytical or convergent thinking. Often related to formal or informal logic and to reasoning.

demonstrating showing children how to do something, how to perform a skill or a technique, how to carry out a process, how to repeat and practise what they have been shown

dialogue shared enquiry between two or more people

enquiry a systematic or scientific process for answering questions and solving problems based on gathering evidence through observation, analysis and reflection

enquiry learning a teaching strategy designed to develop pupils learning through systematic gathering of observation and investigation

enrichment an approach to teaching thinking as separate discrete skills, usually as separate lessons using a particular programme or set of activities

formative assessment assessment which alters subsequent teaching and learning. This may involve teachers in using information gathered in lessons to alter what they do (see **mediation**) or it may also involve the learner through **assessment for learning**.

graphic organizers diagrams which help learners to organize information such as by comparing and contrasting using a grid of similarities and differences

heuristics general or widely applicable problem-solving strategies. Guidelines that generally direct attention, but that do not always produce a correct outcome (see **algorithm**).

higher order thinking evaluation, synthesis and analysis, the higher levels of **Bloom's Taxonomy**

infusion integrating thinking skills teaching into the regular curriculum or lessons; infused programs are commonly contrasted with **enrichment** programs, where separate or discrete skills are taught through lessons to promote thinking.

mediation a teaching strategy where the teacher intervenes and supports the development of pupils' understanding by **modelling** or by direct instruction to help them achieve something they could not do alone

metacognition the process of planning, assessing, and monitoring one's own thinking. Thinking about thinking in order to develop understanding or **self-regulation**.

modelling teaching children in a way that helps them to see the underlying structures, and to understand the embedded or supporting concepts and ideas

multiple intelligences the idea developed by Howard Gardner that IQ does not measure aspects of intelligence sufficiently and that people have strengths in different areas such as visual-spatial or musical as well as more traditionally assessed areas such as linguistic or logico-mathematical

problem based learning an approach using **problem solving** techniques where learners are set specific challenges through realistic or unstructured problems. Similar to **enquiry learning**, but with a particular goal or challenge which needs to be resolved

problem solving a general term which covers a diversity of problem types which make a range of demands on thinking. Some problems have unique solutions and can be tackled with predominantly convergent critical thinking, but many others are open-ended and demand both creative and critical thinking for their solution.

reasoning drawing conclusions or inferences from observations, facts, experiences: deductive inferring conclusions from premises; inductive: inferring a provisional conclusion or hypothesis from information

self-regulation the conscious use of mental strategies to improve thinking and learning, often aimed at particular learning goals

seriation sequencing or arranging objects, ideas or events in a particular order determined by a criterion

Socratic questioning an approach to questioning and discussion where answers to questions are pursued through dialogue

thinking skills 'thinking skills' and related terms are used to indicate a teaching approach which emphasizes the processes of thinking and learning that can be used in a range of contexts. The list of thinking skills in the English National Curriculum is similar to many such lists: information-processing, reasoning, enquiry, creative thinking and evaluation.

transfer the ability to apply an idea or a skill that has been learnt in one context and use it in a different context